Safe

Your complete guide to domestic abuse

by Neville Evans

Safe
Your complete guide to domestic abuse

This Author would like to thank all the people who have helped bring this much needed book to life, special mention goes to Linda Dowi.

The Author would like to thank the following agencies for their kind permission in allowing copy write reproduction. Certain chapters were reproduced by:

Reproduced with kind permission of Women's Aid Federation of England
The Royal College of Psychiatrists
Relate website "paragraph regarding relationship problems"
Respect Website "paragraph regarding perpetrator self referral"
Stonewall Housing
Geshe Kelsang Gyatso "paragraph regarding meditation"
The Home Office
Welsh Assembly Government
Solon Security
Dr Sheila White
Sue Cox from SMART U.K.
CAFCASS

First Edition

Every effort has been made to make this book reflect the most up to date advice. Because developments can vary across the UK, not all advice in this book may be applicable. If you would like to add or comment please contact the author.

Published by Bullied Publishing 2009
137 New Road
Porthcawl
Bridgend
CF36 5DD
www.the-bully.com
Cover Photograph: iStockphoto
Photography : Peter Britton Photography / Solon Security
Design: Neil Edwards (www.akablender.co.uk)

ISBN 978-0-9561434-1-9

About this book

This book has been written specifically for the person who is experiencing domestic abuse from a current or ex-partner. The aim of the book is to help you understand domestic abuse and inform you about the various ways in which you can seek help. The book has been written as a guide that will help you make informed choices, offering support and advice. Domestic Abuse is a complex subject and each persons experience can differ from one day to the next. This book has been written with the help of many people who have survived and moved on from an abusive relationship, it has also been reviewed by many professionals working in this area.

Safety Warning

Do not allow the person who is abusing you to find this book. Please keep it safe or in a place where it will not be recognised. It has been designed not to compromise your safety. If you're an agency worker giving this book to someone in need, do not give it to a person who is continually intoxicated or a person who cannot comprehend the need for its privacy and security. Use your professional wisdom. If you are in immediate danger always call the police, and always dial 999 if it is an emergency.

If you want to talk through the different options, you could call the Freephone 24 hour National Domestic Violence Helpline, run in partnership between Women's Aid and Refuge, on **0808 2000 247**.

The National Domestic Violence Helpline provides emotional and practical support, and information to men and women experiencing (or who have experienced) domestic abuse and to those seeking help on someone else's behalf. Helpline staff will discuss the available options and help you to make an informed choice. If it is appropriate, they may refer you to a refuge, or to outreach services and other sources of help and information. You won't be pushed into making any decision you are not happy with, nor will you be expected to take any steps you don't feel ready for. All calls are taken in the strictest of confidence, and are free of charge wherever you are in the country.

For male victims of abuse (specifically in Wales) Project Dyn **0808 8010 321** and nationally Men's Advice Line 0808 801 0327 and Man Kind **01823 334 244**.

Contents

Useful Local Contacts

Domestic Violence Service's ....

Samaritans ....

Doctors ....

Dentists ....

Community Nurse ....

Drug and Alcohol Support Worker ....

Health Visitor ....

Security Company ....

Sarc Crisis Worker ....

Housing Officer ....

Benefits Adviser ....

Solicitor ....

Victim Care Officer ....

Witness Care Officer ....

Local Court ....

Midwife ....

Social Worker ....

Police Officer ....

Independent Domestic Violence Adviser ....

Counsellor ....

Therapist ....

Debt Advisor ....

Financial Adviser ....

Friend ....

Other ....

1

RELATIONSHIP PROBLEMS AND DOMESTIC ABUSE

ADVICE FOR RELATIONSHIP PROBLEMS

Although they can be painful and unpleasant arguments are common in all kinds of relationships. But disagreements don't have to end in hostile silence or a screaming match. Learning ways of handling discussions on emotive topics and looking out for the patterns and triggers in your arguments can really help you improve the situation.

Find out why you argue

Think about what you're really arguing about. On the surface it could be about money, sex, housework, disciplining children or other family matters. But question what you are really arguing about? It might help you to think about your physical feelings, stress or tiredness can intensify a fight. Or think about how other people's input might fuel your anger.

When you can't stop arguing

If your conflict is rooted in intractable problems, it may be hard, or even impossible, to alter the pattern. If you recognise any of these factors, you need to find support and help, whether from friends, family or getting in touch with a relationship counsellor.

- ❏ Your lives are moving in totally different directions.
- ❏ Alcoholism, drug addiction or other problems feature in your relationship.
- ❏ One of you is having an affair.
- ❏ One of you no longer loves the other, or has actually decided to leave.

How you argue

There are as many ways of having an argument as there are couples who argue. Some common and highly destructive patterns are:

Stonewalling: total withdrawal and refusal to discuss the issue. Partner feels unvalued and unheard.

Criticism: Commenting negatively on the other's behaviour, over and above the current problem. 'You're always so forgetful.' Partner feels attacked and threatened.

Contempt: Sneering, belligerence or sarcasm. 'You think you're so clever.' Partner feels humiliated and belittled.

Defensiveness: Aggressively defending and justifying self to partner. 'You haven't got a clue just how much I have to remember every day.' Partner feels attacked. Row escalates.

Changing the way you tackle rows

Think about the ways you and your partner argue, then think about how you would like to change these. Notice how easily you slip into familiar routines of arguing, almost without thinking. Talk this over with your partner if you can, but if that feels too difficult, go ahead and start changing away. Your partner's reactions will alter in response to yours. Aim for a 'win-win' style of disagreeing, where no one feels they've lost. This will let both partners:

- ❏ outline their own needs.
- ❏ listen to each other's needs.
- ❏ talk flexibly about solutions that give each of them enough of what they want.

Six steps to handling arguments constructively

If you want to raise a tricky topic with your partner, start the discussion amicably. Don't go in with all guns firing, or with a sarcastic or critical comment. For instance,in the example of overspending, say, 'Can we talk about the credit card bill - we needto work out a spending limit that suits us both', not, 'I'm furious about that bill - why do you go over the top every time?'

Try to **understand** your partner's reactions, and remember that you are not just arguing about the 'surface' problem. If your partner says, 'Just let me take care of the money, will you', remember that perhaps in their childhood their role model controlled all household affairs. It will need careful and sensitive negotiation, over a period of time, to alter this pattern of expectations.

Respect your partner's views, even if you are annoyed. Instead of saying, 'I'm not a child!' try, 'I know it's important to you to feel able to spend as and when you like, but I need to have a say in how our money is used, too'.

Take **responsibility** for your own emotions. Why you are so upset? Has something from the past been stirred up by this latest row? Do you fear loss of control in other aspects of your life? Saying, 'You make me so angry…' places the blame for your feelings squarely on to your partner. Yes, his or her behaviour may have triggered your feelings, but their depth may have little to do with the current problem.

Keep tabs on **physical feelings**, which warn you if you are close to losing control. A knot in the stomach, breathlessness, tears, all spell trouble. Leave the room, and taketime to calm down.

Be prepared to **compromise**. Often the only way to reach a win-win solution is for both partners to give some ground. Don't stick rigidly to your desired outcome. Check out what your partner wants to achieve - don't take it for granted that you already know. Then tell him or her what it is you are hoping for, and explore different possibilities together until you reach a solution that both are happy with.

Relate offers advice, relationship counselling, sex therapy, workshops, mediation, consultations and support face-to-face, by phone and through their website.
To contact relate, visit **www.relate.org.uk**
or phone **0300 100 1234.**

Safety Warning

Couples counselling or mediation is not advised if your relationship involves control and violent behavior. However relate produce a number of good books that involve personal relationship development.

WHAT IS DOMESTIC ABUSE?

Domestic Abuse is best described as the use of physical and/or emotional abuse or violence, including undermining of self confidence, sexual violence or the threat of violence, by a person who is or has been in a close relationship. Domestic abuse can go beyond actual physical violence. It can also involve emotional abuse, the destruction of a spouse's or partner's property, their isolation from friends, family or other potential sources of support, threats to others including children, control over access to money, personal items, food, transportation and the telephone, and stalking.

It can also include violence perpetrated by a son, daughter or any other person who has a close or blood relationship with the victim/survivor. It can also include violence inflicted on, or witnessed by, children. The wide adverse effects of living with domestic abuse for children must be recognised as a child protection issue. The effects can be linked to poor educational achievement, social exclusion and to juvenile crime, substance abuse, mental health problems and homelessness from running away.

Domestic abuse is not a "one-off" occurrence; it is frequent and persistent.

Domestic Abuse is also prevalent in Lesbian, Gay, Bi-sexual and Transgender people, however there are subtle differences when considering the type of abuse. There will come a time where by you have tried to adapt and come to realise your current relationship problems tend to sway towards Domestic Abuse. Your partner cannot understand, compromise, listen or take responsibility.

RECOGNISING DOMESTIC VIOLENCE

An argument can be described as a passing thunder storm, with all its ferocity there are always clear skies at the end of the day. Domestic abuse is not such a passing affair, it is like a strong subtle undercurrent that continually swirls and pulls at your mind and body. An undercurrent that eventually pushes you down to the depths of despair.

A healthy relationship has the following qualities: it is a relationship that is consistent and accepts the ups and downs of life.

>*No violence* = passive and loving
>
>*No stealing* = gives and supports the family
>
>*No lying* = trustworthy
>
>*No cheating with others* = committed and respectful
>
>*No breaking up relationships* = supportive, tolerant and helpful. Considers your happiness at all times.

- ❏ Has your partner tried to keep you from seeing your friends or family?
- ❏ Has your partner prevented you from doing things that you enjoy?
- ❏ Does your partner constantly check up on you or ring you constantly?
- ❏ Is your partner jealous?
- ❏ Does your partner constantly belittle or humiliate you, or regularly criticise or insult you in front of other people?
- ❏ Are you frightened of your partner?
- ❏ Have you ever changed your behaviour because you are afraid of what your partner might do or say to you?
- ❏ Has your partner ever smashed an ornament in rage?
- ❏ Has your partner ever hurt or threatened you or your children?
- ❏ Does your partner control the household finances?
- ❏ Has your partner ever forced you to do something that you really did not want to do?
- ❏ Is your partner cruel to the family pet?
- ❏ Has your partner ever threatened to take your children away?
- ❏ Has your partner ever forced you to have sex with him or with other people? Has he or she made you participate in sexual activities that you are uncomfortable about?
- ❏ Is your partner unreasonable and controlling?
- ❏ Does your partner blame his/her use of alcohol or drugs for his/her behaviour?
- ❏ Does your partner impose strict rules with punishment?

If you answered yes to one or more of the above questions, this indicates that you may be experiencing domestic violence.

What Should I Do?

Take a good look in the mirror and say to yourself, "I am not imagining things. This is really happening to me". Acceptance is the first stage to recovery. After the shock has sunk in, and you have acknowledged your distressing set of circumstances, you must tell someone. Believe it or not, so many people living around you know already what is happening in your life. Many people have experienced domestic abuse. You are not alone and will never be. Plan to tell someone you know will listen and understand.

24-hour National Domestic Violence Helpline	**0808 2000 247**
Wales Domestic Abuse Helpline	**0808 80 10 800**
England Domestic Abuse Helpline	**0808 2000 247**
Scottish Domestic Abuse Helpline	**0800 027 1234**
Northern Ireland Domestic Abuse Helpline	**0800 917 1414**

Only you know what to do and only you can make the right decision. It has to come from within. However, there aremany issues that you need to consider and rushing into a decision will only unsettle you. When we are faced with life choices we have to make decisions that may alter the course of our life. Altering our life means that we have to change and as human beings change can be very uncomfortable.

Ask your self some questions. Do you want to be happy? Does your current lifestyle ensure that you and your family are totally happy? Answer these questions with absolute honesty and go with your gut feeling. So many people will tell you what to do. They will say, "I wouldn't put up with that. Just leave them, It's easy!" Your friends are not you. Once you have answered for yourself you have to be prepared to make one of two decisions. You can leave the relationship or you can stay.

Staying In The Relationship

It's difficult staying in a relationship that has no firm foundation. For your relationship to be harmonious **both of you** have to be committed to change. There may be many aspects of your relationship that you may need to explore including your own inner thoughts and feelings. Both of you should be extremely proud that you have endeavoured to improve yourselves. There are many people who can help and support you. It is important to seek advice from independent persons so that you will gain a clearer more balanced perspective. If there has been violence in your relationship, you may need to consider your personal safety.

Safety Warning
Please be aware not all abusers are ready to be helped. If your partner is not ready to seek change, do not tell them about this service. Advising them to change may put you in greater danger.

ADVICE FOR MEN AND WOMEN WHO ADMIT THAT THEY ARE ABUSIVE

People can change. It will take a lot of hard work but it can happen. As long as the abuser take's full responsibility of their actions and commit themselves to changing, it can happen with the right kind of help.

Talk about it

You can start by calling the Respect Phoneline on 0845 122 8609. We can discuss what's been happening and help you understand your situation better. We can also tell you what help is available. Our helpline is confidential and anonymous .

We are open Monday - Friday 10am - 1pm and 2pm - 5pm.

The best kind of help you can get is to join a specialist behaviour-change programme. These programmes are generally called 'domestic violence perpetrator programmes'. They are designed to help men understand and change their abusive/ violent behaviours and develop respectful, non-abusive relationships. They work in small groups of men who have been abusive and/or violent and they want to change. Unfortunately, these programmes are not available everywhere, you can call the Respect Phoneline on 0845 122 8609 to find out if there is one in your area.

Find out more

If you enjoy reading you might want to get hold of this book '**Violent No More**' by **Michael Paymar**, Hunter House Publishers, 2000, ISBN 0897932684

Every perpetrator programme should have an attached service for partners offeringinformation and support. In fact, a perpetrator programme without such a service forthe woman who was suffered the abuse is likely to increase the risks towards her rather than promote her safety.

There are currently no female perpetrator courses being run in the UK, however Respect can help both male and female abusers.

ABUSIVE PSYCHOLOGY

An abuser is a person who holds the belief that they are more important than you are. They hold the opinion that they have the right to manipulate and control your thoughts, appearance and lifestyle. An abuser uses an abuse of power. They will use many different tactics and will insult you, mistreat you and undermine you. They will repeat their actions. The abuser adopts a rigid approach. The abuser's mind is fixed on a set of values and ideas that they believe are real and never change. They believe that these are rules, and rules can never be broken. Our beliefs are the ideas that we have about the world. A belief is something we hold true to ourselves. Beliefs come from all around us; our parents, friends and experiences. We are moulded by the beliefs that we hold. How our beliefs are formed can be very subtle.

The abuser has a very mixed up belief system and tries to apply rational beliefs to different circumstances. Inside the abuser's mind this conflict and confusion leads to frustration.

The abuser's mental disposition is confusing at the best of times. The inner world of the abuser is at the heart of why he or she continues to target you. The unconscious decisions that the abuser makes are a result of a process called "splitting". The abuser when confronted with any outside behaviour, event or personal circumstance, will split the response to this experience into either a "good" or "bad" label.

Splitting is a constant process, and the bully will split everything you say, every action you take and your appearance into either a good response, or in your case a bad response. If the bully continues to hold a "bad" label then there becomes a build up of inner frustration until the bully has to transfer all his or her negativities onto you. This constant labelling then results in bullying behaviour. (Bullying behaviour is described in more detail.) This is very confusing for the person on the receiving end, as sometimes you may notice how they can also be very nice to you. This is because your actions at that time signify a "good" response in their minds. Many people have called this a Jekyll and Hyde personality. For the victim of such behaviour it is worth remembering that you cannot change the "splitting" process, all you can do is adapt to it. The abuser has to recognise the error in his or her thinking patterns and actively change this frustrating process.

The abuser's beliefs are unknown to you. Read the following statements and apply the word "Bad" to each statement.

I am going out for a walk with my friends…

Could you possibly do the cooking tonight?

I am thinking about starting a night class…

I am considering going on holiday with a girlfriend…

Would you look after the children for ten minutes?

Could I invite our friends/parents around tonight?

I am working late tonight, could you put the children to bed?

Notice that these statements are everyday events, however if you apply the word "Bad", your personal frame of reference changes. The cycle of abuse confirms this process and many people recognise a period of tension before the actual abuse starts. The build up of tension is an early warning system, and it should tell you that a great deal of "mental splitting" is racing through the abuser's mind. Some abusers don't show this side of their personality until it's too late. That's why they are labelled with a Jekyll and Hyde personality, and many people don't believe the person experiencing domestic abuse. Why should they be believed? The abuser is such a nice person. Many people suffering abuse don't realise this process and feel very confused. However, when it is explained to them a light bulb illuminates inside their minds.

Society, the media, institutions, sport and governments can reinforce the message that violence and abuse are OK. This is also called perception. Perception is a mix of beliefs, values and how we see the world from our point of view. Where we sometimes go wrong with our understanding of perception is that we are told that it is as a result of what is happening around us. This is a completely mistaken view. Even though outside influences shape our belief system it still remains our own responsibility to make choices about what we believe. The problem the abuser has is that he or she hasn't reflected on this fact and continues to act and behave with no consideration to his or her fellow human beings.

The splitting process creates a personal need for power, mastery and control. The abuser's need is at the heart of why you are being bullied. Situational experiences also deepen the need for power and control.

An abuser is an insecure person who doesn't understand his or her inner feelings. The abuser's world view is a reflection of those feelings. The abuser always believes that it is the other person's fault and that they are the reason for his or her unhappiness. The abuser has a fixed way of thinking and cannot accept people's differences in opinion, culture, religion, and ideas etc. If we adopt a happy flexible belief system then the world outside also appears happy. Christmas Day is a happy day; everyone we meet is happy and joyful. Except the abuser, they didn't get what they wanted. It doesn't matter that his or her whole village is happy. If the abuser does not feel happy inside then nothing else can change that.

A consistent belief system is one that is based on good human qualities: patience, tolerance, kindness, trust, friendship, co-operation, respect and love. Above all it is a belief system that puts other people first and builds a sense of community. When we are happy inside then the world also appears happy.

A abusers belief of self importance comes from deep within him. Self importance can seem real and fixed. When we feel threatened we experience solid resistance in our bodies. Close your eyes and imagine that someone has upset you. If you really think about how you feel you may identify with your inner resistance. If we are deeply upset by someone or something we may feel more resistance. Human beings all feel this inner resistance. Human beings do not want to harbour these inner feelings as we all know that they are no good for us. However, the abuser will choose the quickest and simplest way to get rid of these feelings. The abuser will become angry and when confronted with a difference to his/hers own values and beliefs he/she has to dominate and control. Anger translates into abuse and eventually violence.

Have you noticed that some people argue less, are fun to be around, and seem happier? If you spend more time with these happy people you will come to realise that their outlook is flexible, and they don't consider themselves too important.

The greater amount of self importance you hold about yourself will always translate into greater problems. The abuser has an exaggerated sense of self importance and does not realise that their perception could be wrong.

1 The abuser may use any excuse to punish you, very often you may hear people say, "It's because of your differences". You may be the victim of Domestic Abuse for lots of reasons. Here are some excuses: you are gay, disabled, clever, ambitious, heterosexual, black, white, English, Scottish, stupid, moody, sexy, or talkative, etc. The list goes on and on and it always will go on. Never believe that you are a victim. You are just a normal human being doing your bit in this massively diverse world.

THE WARNING SIGNS OF ABUSE

Jealousy

At the beginning of a relationship an abuser will always say that jealousy is a sign of love. He or she may question you about who you have spoken to or seen during the day, may accuse you of flirting, or be jealous of time you spend with family, friends, children or hobbies which do not include him or her. As the jealousy progresses he or she may call you frequently during the day or drop by unexpectedly. He or she may be unhappy about, or refuse to let you work for fear you'll meet someone else, check the car mileage or ask friends to keep an eye on you. Jealousy is not proof of love; it is a sign of insecurity and possessiveness.

Controlling behaviour

Controlling behaviour is often disguised or excused as concern; concern for your safety, your emotional or mental health, the need to use your time well, or to make sensible decisions. Your abuser may be angry or upset if you are 'late' coming back from work, shopping, visiting friends, etc, even if you told him or her you would be back later than usual. Your abuser may question you closely about where you were, whom you spoke to, the content of every conversation you held, or why you did something he or she was not involved in. As this behaviour gets worse, you may not be allowed to make personal decisions about the house, clothing, or going to church, how you spend your time or money or even make you ask for permission to leave the house or room. Alternately, he or she may allow you your own decisions in theory, but penalise you for making the wrong ones. Concern for our loved ones to a certain extent is normal - trying to control their every move is not.

Quick involvement

Many victims of abuse dated or knew their abuser for less than six months before they were engaged or living together. The abuser will often claim 'love at first sight', that you are 'made for each other', or that you are the only person whom he could ever talk to so openly, feel so at home with, could understand him or her so well. He or she may tell you that they have never loved anyone so much or felt so loved by anyone so much before, when you have really only known each other for a short amount of time. He or she needs someone desperately, and will pressure you to commit to them or make love before you feel the relationship has reached 'that stage'. He or she may also make you feel guilty for not committing yourself to them.

Unrealistic expectations

The abuser may expect you to be the perfect husband, wife, mother, father, lover, and friend. He or she is very dependent on you for all their needs, and may tell you they can fulfil all your needs as lover, friend, and companion. Statements such as: *'If you love me . . .', 'I'm all you need . . .', 'You are all I need . . .'*, are common. Your abuser may expect you to provide everything for him or her emotionally, practically, financially or spiritually, and then blame you for not being perfect or living up to expectation.

Isolation

The abuser may try to curtail your social interaction. He or she may prevent you from spending time with your friends or family and demand that you only go places 'together'. They may accuse you of being 'tied to your mother's apron strings', not being committed to the relationship, or view people who are your personal friends as 'causing trouble' or 'trying to put a wedge' between you. They may want to live in the country without a phone, not let you use the car, stop you from working or gaining further education or qualifications.

Blame-shifting for problems

Very rarely will an abusive personality accept responsibility for any negative situation or problem. If they are unemployed, can't hold down a job, were thrown out of college or university or fall out with their family, it is always someone else's fault, be it the boss, the government, or their mother. They may feel that someone is always doing them wrong, or is out to get him. He or she may make a mistake and then blame you for upsetting them or preventing them from doing as they wished to.

Blame-shifting for feelings

The abuser will deny feelings stem from within him or her but see them as reactions to your behaviour or attitude toward them. He or she may tell you that; *'you make me mad', 'you're hurting me by not doing what I ask'*, or that they cannot help feeling mad, upset, etc. Feelings may be used to manipulate you, ie *'I would not be angry if you didn't ...'.* Positive emotions will often also be seen as originating outside the abuser, but are more difficult to detect. Statements such as *'You make me happy'*, or *'You make me feel good about myself'*, are also signs that the abuser feels you are responsible for their sense of well-being. Either way, you become in his or her mind the cause of good and bad feelings and are therefore responsible for their emotional well-being and happiness. Consequently, you are also to blame for any negative feelings such as anger, upset or depression.

Hypersensitivity

Most abusers have very low self-esteem and are therefore easily insulted or upset. They may claim their feelings are 'hurt' when they are really angry, or take unrelated comments as personal attacks. They may perceive normal set-backs (having to work additional hours, being asked to help out, receiving a parking fine, etc.) as grave personal injustices. They may view your preference for something which differs from their own as a criticism of their taste and therefore themselves (eg blue wallpaper rather than pink, etc.).

Rigid Gender Roles

Abusers usually believe in stereotypical gender roles. A man may expect a woman to serve him; stay at home, obey him in all things - even things that are criminal in nature. A male abuser will often see women as inferior to men, more stupid, unable to be a whole person without a relationship. Female abusers may expect the man to provide for them entirely, shift the responsibility for her well-being onto him or heckle him as being 'not a real man' if he shows any weakness or emotion.

Verbal Abuse

In addition to saying things that are meant to be cruel and hurtful, either in public or in private, this can include degrading remarks or running down any accomplishments. Often the abuser will tell you that you are 'stupid', or could not manage without them. They may keep you up all night to 'sort this out once and for all' or even wake you at night to continue to verbally abuse you. The abuser may even say kindly things to your face, but speak badly about you to friends and family.

LGBT Abuse

The victims of LGBT domestic abuse may experience all of the above behaviours. However there are a number of subtle differences. These include: the threat of 'outing' one's sexual orientation to people who don't know or understand LGBT issues. The threat may include divulging personal information to close family members, work colleagues, religious groups, extremist groups etc. The threat of using this information acts as a way of controlling their victim. This type of behaviour is also known as blackmail.

LEAVING THE RELATIONSHIP

Take a deep breath and be prepared for change. Take every day as it comes and do not plan too far ahead. It is hard but it will be worth it in the end. There are so many people who can support you and want to support you. There are many agencies that are there solely for you. To say 'I'm leaving you' is very hard, even when a relationship has been in trouble for some time. The difficulty increases beyond measure if there has been a history of violence between you and your partner.

Perhaps you have already tried to leave and so you are only too aware of what the reaction from your partner will be. So how can you leave? First of all, the time has to be right. After considering the advantages and disadvantages of leaving. You must be desperate enough to be determined to go.

This book will guide you along the path to many people who understand your set of circumstances, if you are considering leaving, your first consideration will be a safe place to live and sleep. If there has been violence in your relationship, you may need to consider your personal safety.

CHAPTER SUMMARY

❑ *Keep tabs on your inner feelings, if your feelings become unbearable, leave the area, and give yourself time to cool down.*

❑ *It's not your fault. You cannot change an abusive personality.*

❑ *Abuse involves jealousy, control and isolation. Abuse is about power and control.*

❑ *If your partner is ready to be helped and admits being abusive, contact the respect phone line.*

PERSONAL
SAFETY

2

2 Safety planning in an abusive relationship

In an abusive relationship your personal safety is at risk. The abuser's personality is unpredictable at first, however, the longer you stay, the more predictable it may become. It is important to try and see a pattern; what triggers the abuser to act in a particular way. In essence this form of personal flexibility (you are adapting to the abuser's outbursts) becomes a subtle form of control (you are changing your behaviour because of abusive behaviour). Please don't become stubborn. Remember planning your safety allows you to have an element of flexibility and control. You are managing an abusive situation and successfully stopping more physical abuse.

Safety plans need to be considered as if you were planning for a fire alarm. Read through each plan and walk through your home spotting the potential hazards. Move to different areas of your home and try and imagine what you would do if you were attacked. Visualise the steps that you would take and the things that you would do. This allows it to be an automatic response if the inevitable happens.

THE THREAT OF VIOLENCE

When we are confronted with the threat of violence we can become scared or angry. You will notice many swirling feelings within your body. You may feel extremely nervous with butterflies in your stomach. Some people feel sick and paralysed with fear. All these feelings are perfectly normal. This is an aspect of fear called the fight or flight response. Evolution has prepared you for the threat of violence. Your prehistoric brain has developed a natural response to the threat of violence. Thousands of years ago our ancestors relied on this response daily. Our ancestors had to avoid predators and fight with warring tribes. Your body is preparing to run or fight.

Unfortunately the threat of violence is still with us today, however, it is small when we compare it to what our ancestors had to go through. Our brain transmits messages to the adrenal glands. These special glands release adrenaline. The hormone adrenaline is a special transmitter and travels around the body in an instant. It makes your heart beat quicker, your breathing rate increases, you become stronger and your tolerance to pain increases. Your reactions become faster and you can run and jump further. You are ready for action.

Sometimes when our abuser torments us this natural reaction can have the reverse effect. You may become more agitated and stressed. Sometimes this can make the situation worse. If you feel yourself getting uptight and nervous take some deep breaths and say to yourself, "It is normal to feel like this". You will remain calmer. Fear is only natural, as such try and control your fear and remain receptive to the events unfolding in front of you.

What is happening to the abuser prior to becoming violent?

The abuser at this point is going through a period of intense anger. The abuser loses all mental control. The abuser's mind is making the situation worse, repeating and re-living all the anger and frustration. However, if you remain calm in a confrontational situation you are in control. Being able to think is the key to diffusing conflict and avoiding violence.

Learn the signs of violence coming. Does your abuser complain about stress at work, criticise your dress sense, drink more alcohol or behave secretly? Try and notice changes in your partner's behaviour before they go into a violent rage. Write down your observations. These subtle clues will allow you time to plan an escape. ever make an assumption about violence, it usually builds and gets worse with time.

RECOGNISING CONFRONTATION

Situational awareness

Ask the following questions: Where is your partner? What room are you in? What state of mind are they in?

The stare

The abuser will hold a stare across the room, and is looking for you to catch his/her gaze. This stage of awareness is an opportunity for you to avoid confrontation. Do not make it obvious but keep a watch over the abuser.

The question

If you have been indecisive and have not avoided the abuser, you are ready for the next stage of confrontation. Your abuser is going to project feelings of inadequacy onto you and make you the problem. They will say, "Have You Got A Problem With Me?". What they are really saying is, "I am insecure, and I have a problem with you". Be aware that at this stage the abuser has already planned to attack you. The abuser may attack you verbally or physically, depending on the circumstances.

The body language

Body language will change as the situation escalates. Even at the first stage look for the vital signs of body language that demonstrates violence. Communication is mostly through body language. They will get closer to you. The following description is equally applicable to men and women. Your abuser's chest will be inflated like a balloon, and arms will puff outwards like a bird. They will stand tall and appear robotic. When talking they will use hands and point in a stabbing motion. The face will redden, eyes will bulge, and teeth may show. The jaw will tighten and they will appear bigger. The abuser will constantly look around and may stamp the floor.

The provocation

Here it becomes increasingly tense. The abuser will mutter words like, "Yeah, yeah, so, so". At this stage it will be almost impossible to communicate with them. What the abuser is doing is target picking. The provocation can last some time depending on the abuser. A violent abuser will build up to this stage in a matter of split seconds. They will also swear at you.

The Attack

The distance between you and the abuser will shorten and they may look for an opportunity to attack. This will depend your own body language. The majority of attackers are right-handed and right-footed. Do you know if your abuser is right- or left-handed? In most cases your abuser is going to throw a right-hand hooking punch to the head. This isn't always the case as some like to grab and pull your hair.

What Can I Do About It?

You cannot change an abuser, only an abuser can do that. You have to adapt to the abuser's behaviour and make quick decisions.

Situational Awareness

Keep your head up and look around you, and every now and again look behind you. Gather information, and use your eyes and ears. Anticipate problems before they arise. Think Safety **PLAN**. Think **VULNERABILITY**.

Plan

Now that I have given an explanation of the stages of a violent confrontation, consider the following safety planning advice.

- ❏ Don't drink alcohol together as the probability of a violent attack increases. If he or she insists, try and pour some lemonade into your drink. Alcohol reduces your ability to run, defend yourself and escape.

- ❏ You cannot reason with a drunk person. Don't try to tell them what to do. If they are starting to pick on you then make the decision for them and get out of their way.

- ❏ Keep them fed and watered. Why on earth would someone tell me to do this? Simply; physiological stress has a major impact on the brain. If someone has the abusing personality and they are hungry and drunk, then probability of violence increases ten fold. If they are drinking alcohol make sure they eat something too. It will stop them from getting really drunk. It may help you.

- ❏ Plan your safety around sporting events. If he/she is a sporting fan, consider when his/her team are playing. When the abuser's team wins, the probability of violence, believe it or not increases. If he/she is going drinking all day with the friends, plan to stay with a family member or close friend.

- ❏ Pack a getaway suitcase and include all the family essentials: money, passports, birth certificates, cheque book, bank cards, identification, keys for your house, keys for work, legal documents, prescription drugs, clothing, benefit books and your driving licence. In extreme cases get copies of these important documents.

- ❏ Replicate important keys and documents and keep them somewhere safe.

- ❏ Work out a signal system with a neighbour or friend, consider a code word to tell the children to leave.

- ❏ Teach your children to call 999 in an emergency.

- ❏ Don't stay and face the violence. Seek help from a friend or neighbour, and get the children out of the house. Park your car in such a way that you are not blocked in by your partners car.

- ❏ Consider purchasing a Howsar quick lock. This handy lock will give you time to get away. The portable lock allows you to lock a door in a short amount of time. Employ a diversionary tactic first "I am putting some make up on or I am getting you a beer from the fridge". Lock the escape door and get out of the house.

- ❏ Keep your mobile on you at all times and make sure it has sufficient credit. You can get a prefix security number for your phone. For example if you press and hold 3, then your mobile will ring 999 or a security company. Another good idea, is to silently ring 999, keep the phone off the receiver and if he gets near to you start shouting. Police services in the UK will respond immediately to such incidents.

- ❏ Add in your mobile phone a list of useful telephone numbers e.g. solicitor, doctor, crisis centre, etc. Put these contacts under your friends' names.

- ❏ There are also imitation keep safe's on the market, that will allow you to hide money and important documents etc.

Think vulnerability

- ❏ If the abuser is becoming aggressive then stay away from the kitchen and garage. There are many implements that could be used as weapons and cause serious injury.

- ❏ It sounds silly but put things away, e.g. children's toys, they may prevent you from escaping and they can also be used as weapons.

- ❏ Place knives and scissors in hard to reach places. Get rid of the counter top knife rack. If the abuser asks say "Its for the children's safety".

- ❏ Ornaments can also be dangerous e.g. It's amazing how many people own samurai swords etc.

- ❏ If your partner owns a gun, keep ammunition separate from the actual weapon.

- ❏ Consider purchasing an emergency life hammer. This article can be kept in a small handbag and used to smash glass in an emergency.

- ❏ Animals can seriously add to a violent household, for example pit bull dogs get very agitated in violent encounters. They pose a very real risk to all your family.

- ❏ Don't go upstairs because many people are thrown down them. Avoid places where you could be trapped as they may lock you inside.

- ❏ Your vulnerable when you are combing your hair, using hair straigtners or cleaning with acid based products.

- ❏ Does your partner keep petrol on the premises? Dispose of it discreetly.

MANAGING CONFRONTATION

The stare

It is absolutely normal to avoid confrontation and aggression - avoid the abuser and leave the area. There are many factors to consider at this stage. Is he or she bigger and more aggressive than you? Has he or she been drinking alcohol? Does they have a history of violence? Prepare yourself if your sixth sense starts to answer "yes" to these questions. Do you have a panic alarm handy? Where are you going to run?

Consider trickery

The abuser may try and entice you into what is called a deceptive attack. What they will do is ask a stupid question and then attack you. (This is a technique that distracts and confuses you).

EXAMPLES

> **Bully :** What's the time?
> **Abused :** Looks at her watch and is distracted
> **Bully:** Attacks, and slaps you across the face.

> **Bully :** Let me stroke your hair, I am sorry I did those things.
> **Abused :** Guard is dropped,
> **Bully:** Attacks and pulls her hair.

> **Bully :** You look really sexy when you stand like that?
> **Abused :** Stands in a vulnerable position
> **Bully:** Attacks easily.

The question "HAVE YOU GOT A PROBLEM WITH ME?"

If your bully comes close then step away, keep your hands up, and turn your palms outwards. Stand at a 45 degree angle. Tuck your chin in and talk at a distance. Move side to side when talking to them. Say to them firmly; *"NO, I DON'T WANT TROUBLE. I DON'T WANT TO FIGHT."* Don't turn your back on them and keep to the wall. Appear to give in to them. Remember that by complying with their rules you are giving them a sense of control. You are also playing for time and preparing to respond.

The body language

Appear non-confrontational and keep your hands and palms facing outwards. This is a ploy as it tells the abuser you are not willing to fight and gives them a sense of power. Tell them what they want to hear and keep on saying it even if it is, *"I am sorry, I am sorry"*. Give them power.

Many women who have been beaten by their partners sometimes say it is best to say very little. By saying very little you do not add to the problem (in his or her mind). Every case is different and you will be the best person to decide.

The provocation

Do not argue and try to remain calm. Keep well away from them. They are dangerous but you have options: you can run away, you can activate your panic alarm or you can defend yourself.

The attack

If you are getting attacked keep moving away from them. Cover your face and try and protect yourself. Do not let them get too close. Keep on shouting, *"HELP, HELP, STOP, and STOP."*

LEAVING YOUR ABUSER AND YOUR PERSONAL SAFETY

Preparing to leave

It is not your fault; it is always the abuser's problem. You have been extremely brave. You have tried, you have adapted, and you have loved and forgiven. After all your efforts you cannot change them. It is going to be a difficult time, but it will not last forever. Be comforted in the knowledge that you have made a decision that will affect generations of your family, ensuring that you are happier and contented. When planning to leave your abuser, take your time and break each decision into manageable daily amounts. Take a good look at your diary and pick a time and date when your abuser is most distracted or easily confused. For example: Does your abuser work away from home? Does your abuser suffer from hang over's? (Early morning, when they are asleep) Is there an event that they must attend? When you do leave, try and make your home as normal as possible. When you do leave remember that abusers are particularly dangerous after you have left, be cautions in your every move.

After your relationship has ended a critical period usually follows. This is when emotions are heightened and there is a period of loss that both experience. There may be a period of pestering, it may be that your ex-partner is actually stalking you. If you are being stalked you need to contact the police immediately. You are in particular danger if your ex-partner has a problem with alcohol or drug abuse. Stalking is a serious matter, if you feel

frightened you must tell the police about your fears. If you see your ex-partner more than two occasions within a week, make that phone call. Leave the area immediately and do not attempt to speak to the abuser.

If you have to be at a fixed appointment and you cannot miss the appointment, consider contacting the person and explain your circumstances. You may have to tell the head teacher at your children's school that you are expecting trouble at the school gates. Ask the head teacher to remove your children at a more convenient time.

What decisions will I have to make?

Beginning to think independently will allow you to explore some of the new decisions you will have to make. Don't be overwhelmed by this process, it's about time you were allowed to make decisions, as often your abuser made the important choices. Here are some questions you may want to ask:

Housing

Where are you going to live?
Could you stay with family or friends?
Would you move into a secure local refuge?

Employment

What are your rights and entitlements to special leave?
Who should I tell at work?
Who can I trust?

Finances

How much money do you have saved?
How do you share your savings?

Support

How are you eating?
How is your health?
What are you doing to make yourself feel better?
What support groups are there?

Miscellaneous

Who can you delegate / rely upon?
Who will support you?
What happens if . . . ?

2 What to pack if you are planning to leave your partner

Ideally, you need to take all the following items with you if you leave. Some of these items you can try to keep with you at all times; others you may be able to pack in your "emergency bag".

- ❏ Some form of identification.
- ❏ Birth certificates for you and your children.
- ❏ Passports (including passports for all your children), visas and work permits.
- ❏ Money, bankbooks, cheque book and credit and debit cards.
- ❏ Keys for house, car, and place of work. (You could get an extra set of keys cut, and put them in your emergency bag.)
- ❏ Cards for payment of Child Benefit and any other welfare benefits you are entitled to.
- ❏ Driving licence (if you have one) and car registration documents, if applicable.
- ❏ Prescribed medication.
- ❏ Copies of documents relating to your housing tenure, e.g. mortgage details or lease and rental agreements.
- ❏ Insurance documents, including national insurance number.
- ❏ Address book.
- ❏ Family photographs, your diary, jewellery, small items of sentimental value.
- ❏ Clothing and toiletries for you and your children.
- ❏ Your children's favourite small toys.

You should also take any documentation relating to the abuse - for example police reports, court orders such as injunctions and restraining orders, and copies of medical records if you have them.

Protecting yourself after you have left

After you have left your ex-partner, you may want to think about and anticipate confrontation before it arises. Where will your ex-partner go and who will they speak to. Identify the people who your ex-partner may want to speak to. If you choose to tell those closest to you, ask them to record the times and dates of your ex-partners movements. If you tell supportive people about your circumstances, they can be more prepared to offer support, such as arranging childcare, emotional support and transportation. Importantly limit or monitor your children's access to social net-working sites and email. Talk to your children and explain that they may need to act decisively if a crisis arises. Be aware that ex-partners can be very deceptive and may use many different means to try and manipulate you. These include: trickery, emotional blackmail and the severe threat of violence.

If you have left home but are staying in the same town or area, then these are some of the ways in which you might be able to increase your safety:

DAILY ROUTINE

- ❏ If you have fixed appointments that your partner is aware of, change the time and location.

- ❏ If you have moved and you don't want him to find out where you live, you can ask for the electoral role register to be anonymous.

- ❏ If you have moved away from your area, and don't want your abuser to know where you are, then you need to take particular care with anything that may indicate your location; for example:

- ❏ Your mobile phone could be "tracked"; this is only supposed to happen if you have given your permission, but if your partner has had access to your mobile phone, he could have sent a consenting message purporting to come from you. If you think this could be the case, you should contact the company providing the tracking facility and withdraw your permission; or if you are in any doubt, change your phone.

- ❏ Make sure that your address does not appear on any court papers. (If you are staying in a refuge, they will advise you on this.)

- ❏ If you need to phone your abuser (or anyone with whom he is in contact), make sure your telephone number is untraceable by dialling 141 before ringing.

- ❏ Be aware your partner may report you missing and get the police to find you. Explain to the officer that you have left as a result of Domestic Abuse and you do not want your new address being given out.

- ❏ Talk to your children about the need to keep your address and location confidential.

- ❏ Ask for an ex-directory telephone number.

- ❏ Never answer the door unless you know who is the other side.

- ❏ Lock the doors and windows of your home.

- ❏ Anniversaries are worth considering, an emotional event may trigger a certain behaviour.

- ❏ Can you be sure that your car has not been tracked. Does your partner have the financial means to hire a private detective?

Personal Safety Advice Going Out and About

Personal Attack Alarms are another device that you may consider using in a confrontational situation. They are best used in order to try and disorientate the abuser. Place the alarm near the abuser's face and shout as loud as you can. The abuser will become disorientated and this should give you time to escape.

Technology can help you stay safe. 3ARC Limited have developed a number of safety products that allow you to contact help and support at the touch of a button. The 3ARC Angel system connects your mobile phone to a 24hr dedicated response service using a predefined 0871 number. When your body releases adrenaline fine motor skills become very difficult. The 3ARC system allows you to contact the control centre by speed dialling the number 3 on your mobile phone. Once you have made contact with the control centre your personal details and history will be shown to the operator. The operator will then be able to summon help from a variety of sources including family members, neighbours or the police..

3ARC also offer a GPS locating system know as Track and Talk. This system acts as a mobile phone, when you activate the handset the control operator will be able to speak to you and pinpoint your exact location. Your personal details will be accessed and the appropriate help will be notified. This technology could save you from immanent danger.

Consider the following advice:

- ❑ Keep to main routes and avoid places of darkness. Stick to well lit and busy areas. Plan your route and stick to areas where there is CCTV.

- ❑ Try and vary your times and locations when travelling. Often your abuser will be waiting for you.

- ❑ Keep plenty fuel in your car at all times.

- ❑ When you leave your home, tell someone where you are going, when you will be returning and how you can be contacted. Leave a timetable of your likely whereabouts with loved ones.

- ❑ Carry a mobile phone and make sure it has enough credit on it.

- ❑ Shout 'fire' rather than 'help' as it can get more results. If he starts to chase you, bang on every door possible in the street and draw attention to your self.

- ❑ Try and use the mirrors of cars and reflections of shop windows -- that way you can see what is behind you.

- ❑ When out walking, you should avoid using your mobile phone or texting on the go. This distraction can stop you from being aware of your surroundings. Similarly listening to your iPod whilst walking can limit your awareness.

- ❑ Do not get drunk, you will not be able to think clearly and act decisively.

- ❑ Avoid dark gloomy places, subways, bridges, open fields and dark lanes. Never take a short cut.

Consider what you are wearing and what you are carrying

Depending on the social occasion consider what type of clothing could be a hindrance. Avoid poor foot wear; you can't run with flip flops or high heels. Avoid wearing hoodies and large anoraks as they may block your peripheral vision and can easily be used to stop you seeing. Jewellery can be used to strangle, and (expensive) earrings can easily be ripped out of your skin and can cause injury. Long hair can be used as a tool to grapple with, so tie it up. Keep expensive personal items to a minimum; do you really need your iPod, camera, mobile, laptop, etc? When carrying a rucksack carry it on one shoulder so that if you sense there may be trouble you can dump it and run. Consider wearing sunglasses in the daytime as that way you can avoid eye contact and check out what is going on.

DRIVING

- ❑ Keep your car in good condition and try not to run out of petrol.

- ❑ Try to park in well lit or busy areas, and if you park during the day think about what the area will feel like after dark.

- ❑ If you break down on the motorway follow the arrows to the nearest phone. do not cross the carriageway. wait outside your car (as far away as possible from the carriageway) unless you feel threatened, in which case you should sit in the passenger seat.

- ❑ Lock the car's doors when you get into the vehicle.

- ❑ Use your electronic key fob in the correct way. if you press the key once it will only open the driver's door.

- ❑ Do not give lifts to or accept lifts from people you do not know, or do not know very well.

TAXIS

- ❑ If you are going to be out late, or don't want to travel on public transport on your own, try to arrange a lift home with someone you know or make your journey by taxi.

- ❑ Get to know your local driver, and take his or her personal mobile number - that way you can ring them if you need help.

- ❑ You should always ensure that you travel in a licensed taxi by checking the vehicle's signage or plate and the driver's badge; you should never agree to travel in an unlicensed vehicle with an unlicensed driver.

- ❑ If you pre-book your taxi make a note of the company you are using, and the telephone number, and if possible leave it with a friend.

- ❑ When you get to your destination ask the driver to wait until you are inside.
- ❑ If travelling alone always sit behind the driver in the back seat.
- ❑ If you feel uneasy ask to be let out in a well lit area where there are plenty of people.
- ❑ If in any doubt make an excuse and don't get in the vehicle.

PERSONAL INFORMATION AND CYBER ABUSE

Personal information is information that you give freely about yourself on a website, social networks, emails, text messages and chat rooms. There are many positives to this way of communication; it is cheap, fast and effective. However, there are many downsides and this new age of communication can make abuse worse. You have to decide which method of communication best suits you and weigh up the pros and cons.

The written word can be misinterpreted very easily. Communication is 80% non-verbal, as our body language, tone of voice and presence give a true indication of what we are really saying.

Social networking sites, email and text messages

Communicating this way can be very impersonal as your audience cannot understand how you are feeling. An abuser can pass on all sorts of information on the web about you, and a hate campaign can form. After leaving an abusive partner it is advisable to avoid such ways of communication.

- ❑ Don't put your personal email, mobile telephone number or address on the site.
- ❑ Don't give people ammunition and tell the whole world what you like and dislike; your abuser will have an even stronger advantage, for example he or she may even know where you are going. The other thing to think about is the issue of jealousy. If he or she finds out that you have met someone else they may act even more irrationally.
- ❑ Don't just add friends just for the sake of it.
- ❑ If you are receiving threatening text messages from your abuser then store them on your phone; if they continue and you receive further hoax calls, change your number.
- ❑ Store and save threatening emails.
- ❑ Do not respond to threatening messages.

BANK ACCOUNT SAFETY

If you have just left your abusive partner and you have a joint bank account then it may be safer not to use it, if you do not want him orher to know where you are. Any withdrawals from cash machines or bank branches will be traceable. Use of a joint credit card is also best avoided. Even if you have an account in your sole name statements posted to your home address could be opened by your abuser.

CHANGING YOUR NAME

You can change your name legally using the **Deed Poll** service. You don't need a solicitor's help, and the process can either be completed online or by post. There is a fee for changing your name by Deed Poll, and you might also have to pay for some replacement documents such as a new passport and driving licence.

For more information, visit www.deedpoll.org.uk or call 0800 7833048

KEEPING YOUR HOME SAFE

Considering your basic home security is a must following repeated harassment and stalking from your ex-partner.

You could also consider the following:

- ❑ Purchasing an electronic motion alarm. These handy alarms can be placed near a window or secured next to a vulnerable rear door.

- ❑ The perimeter wall around your home can be secured by the use of a 'Prikka-Strip' and anti climbing paint.

- ❑ Clear all hedges and green areas as they can provide hiding places for "stalkers".

- ❑ Changing the locks on all doors; lock all doors and make sure that your children get into this worthwhile habit.

- ❑ Consider getting a dog.

- ❑ Adding a door viewer to the front door.

- ❑ Installing a digital door eye. This clever device will photograph each visitor to your home and can be used as evidence.

- ❑ Dummy CCTV camera's are cheaper than the real thing and can provide a real deterrent.

- ❑ There are numerous CCTV systems on the market. Make sure that prior to installing the cameras the system is checked in the dark. Patio and street lights can sometimes obscure the view and quality of the camera.

- [ ] Put locks on all windows if you don't have them already.
- [ ] Installing smoke detectors on each floor, and providing fire extinguishers.
- [ ] Installing an outside light (back and front) which comes on automatically when someone approaches.
- [ ] Fix a reinforced door chain on the front door.
- [ ] Lock all doors.
- [ ] Reinforce all internal doors, with bolts and dead-locks.
- [ ] Inform the neighbours that your partner no longer lives there, and asking them to tell you - or call the police - if they see him/her nearby.
- [ ] Use an answering machine to screen calls.

WORK SECURITY

- [ ] If you are a lone worker ask to be enrolled with a g.p.s. monitoring system.
- [ ] Tell your employer about your domestic problems, ask always to be working with another colleague.
- [ ] Pay attention to suspicious packages that have been sent to you for collection.

BANK ACCOUNT SAFETY

- [ ] Remove your personal address from company databases.
- [ ] Write to credit reference agencies and be sure to inform them that you have parted (just in case the abuser tries to apply for credit and render you bankrupt).

CHAPTER SUMMARY

- [ ] *Learn the warning signs of violence and confrontation .*
- [ ] *Anticipate confrontation and leave the area.*
- [ ] *Alcohol and drug use, decreases your opportunities for safety and increase the likelihood for violence.*
- [ ] *Remove all weapons from your home.*
- [ ] *PLAN your safety.*
- [ ] *Remove all items that could be used to strangle / choke or smother you.*

All personal safety products listed within this book can be purchased from www.the-bully.com - Consider your online safety when ordering.

3

WRITING ABOUT YOUR EXPERIENCES

3 Writing about your experiences

Domestic Abuse is a personal experience that is hard to describe. Many people are unaware of the types of behaviour and actions that constitute abuse. We sometimes minimise behaviour saying it was just an argument or a "one off". Excuses are made for someone's behaviour, and over the months and years this behaviour can serve to delude us into thinking that it is normal. It isn't normal behaviour, and the effects are far reaching. Whilst we experience trauma our mind can play tricks with us, and serve to mask our traumatic experiences. When exposed to traumatic experiences our subconscious mind will blot out the actual experience. However the devastating experience is still held in our subconscious mind.

We are unaware of how our experience starts to impact on our everyday experiences, for example, we may get flash backs, we may feel we cannot remember certain dates and times, we may feel upset and scared for no apparent reason. If you have come to the stage whereby you have asked for help from the legal profession then it will come to the stage where you are asked to provide a statement. In your present capacity it may become difficult to remember the actual events that have occurred. Living with an abusive partner is very confusing.

Whatever stage you are at it is important to write about your experiences. You may not like to write you may feel that you wish to draw instead.

Warning

If you start to write about your experiences, keep all your notes in a safe place. Consider keeping them away from your home, for example at a friend's home or at work. Do not let your abuser know about this information.

Writing about your experiences has many benefits including:

- ❑ Identifying a pattern to your abuser's violent behaviour, and seeing the trigger events that lead to violence.

- ❑ Expressing yourself in a therapeutic sense.

- ❑ Seeing the scale of abuse and confirming it isn't your fault.

- ❑ When you are ready this information could help you when you contact the police or a solicitor.

- ❑ It could be used to support you in future proceedings, for example childcare, or divorce proceedings.

WRITING A PERSONAL DIARY

Start your diary with the time and date of the incident. Write about the day; something that will trigger your memory. For example was it someone's birthday or a recognised holiday? It doesn't matter what you write about. It is only there to help you remember.

Make some notes before writing your diary. When you make your notes break each aspect of the incident into small sections. Put each section into small circles and apply the following questions: who, what, why, where, when, and how. Once you have answered each question move onto the next section. The smaller you break each part down the more detailed your diary will become. Once you have a plan stand back and leave it alone for a couple of hours. Return to your notes after you have been refreshed and repeat the entire process again. Now write your story in small simple sentences. Remember to use descriptive words and do not leave any details out.

Include the following information in your personal diary:

- ❑ **Amount** of time (when the incident started and finished)
- ❑ **Distance** (how far you were away from the abuser?)
- ❑ **Visibility** (what were the lighting conditions like; was it night or day; how well you could see the abuser?)
- ❑ **Obstructions** (was there anything obstructing your view?)
- ❑ **Known or seen before** (how do you know the abuser)

POSTERS / GRAFFITI

In certain circumstances abusers may publicise malicious words about you. They may spray graffiti outside your home, on your property or publicise something personal via a poster. Take a picture of the poster with your digital camera. Ask someone else to witness the position of the poster and ask the witness to sign their name on the bottom right hand corner. Make sure you include the time and date. Remove the picture carefully. Make sure you remove it wearing gloves and place it in a large envelope. Do not touch the poster or show it to anybody else. Record the time and date you removed the poster and sign the envelope accordingly. Write a dairy entry about the poster. You can draw diagrams or use maps/plans in order to illustrate your point of view.

TEXT MESSAGE'S

If you have received an abusive text message there are many things you can do. Firstly do not respond to the text message. Write out the text message on a piece of paper, sign and date it. It should read something like this: on Wednesday 14 August at 2200 hours I received a text message from the mobile number 12345678910. I know this to be ****** phone. It was sent to my phone number 10987654321. This mobile phone is owned by me and I am an Easy Telecoms customer. The text message said, "YOU ARE TREADING ON THIN ICE, IT'S GOING TO CRACK". I did not reply to this message.

Repeat the procedure with each text message. Ask a witness to read the messages and ask them to sign each written diary entry. Save each message on your phone's SIM card. Remove the SIM card and keep it for safe keeping. Purchase a new SIM card and consider changing your mobile phone number. You also need to evidence how you obtained your abuser's mobile phone number. Include when and where you exchanged mobile phone numbers.

EMAIL

Save the email on your computer or on a removable memory stick or CD. Print the email using your computer and show it to a witness. Write the date and time on the printout and sign the document. Keep the email somewhere safe and hand it to the person dealing with your case at the earliest possible time. Make a diary entry of what happened; include how you felt when you opened the email. Do not respond to abusive emails.

PACKAGE'S

If your abuser sends you a package in the post try to resist handling the item as you may lose vital forensic evidence. Typically old photographs and damaged personal items have been sent in the post. Do not let anyone else touch the item. Ring the police immediately and pass the item to the police. You could also take a photograph of the item - specifically where you found it. Write about this incident in your personal diary.

BEING SPAT AT

If someone has spat at you, you need to preserve the evidence. If you do remove it keep the tissue that has the saliva on it. Place the saliva in a brown bag and seal it. Record on the bag who spat at you, the time and date. You could take a photograph of the saliva on your face. This is not always practical as the first thing you want to do is remove it.

PHOTOGRAPHS

If you have been assaulted make sure you take photographs of your injuries after the incident. The police may also take photographs of your injuries. You could consider taking photographs a number of days later, as bruising and swelling tend to show more prominently after a few days. If you take digital photographs be sure to save the photographs on a CD-ROM or memory stick. Keep this information safe. Try and make sure that you record the time and date of when and where the photographs were taken. If a friend has witnessed your injuries, again, record the time and date when they saw you. Record who the witnesses are.

MOBILE PHONE VOICE RECORDING

If you have received an abusive phone message there are many things you can do. Firstly do not respond to the message. Write out the message on a piece of paper, sign and date it. Ask a witness to listen to the message and ask them to sign your diary and confirm that this message was abusive. Speak to someone who can help you save the message. Messages can be saved on a portable recording device such as a dictaphone. You could speak to your phone provider about changing your telephone number.

COMPUTER MESSAGES

Today's cyber world involves the use of social networking sites. If you are receiving abusive messages via a site, again, don't respond and save the messages. It is advisable to avoid this type of communication until matters have settled down.

YOUR HOME

If your abuser has ransacked your home and assaulted you, you may have to call the police. Before the police arrive do not clean up the mess, but leave everything as it is. You may want to take photographs of the damage. If there is blood on the floor or in a room do not clean it up. This type of evidence is best photographed.

BEING ASSAULTED

If you have been assaulted you need to get medical treatment and get your injuries medically recorded. Whilst at the doctor's or hospital ask for the name of the person treating you and record this information in your diary.

STALKING

If you are being watched and followed you really need to consider your personal safety. Revert back to the chapter "Personal Safety" for tips and advice. Always carry a mobile phone or a small digital camera. Do not overtly take photographs of the abuser. This may act as a catalyst for an escalation of violence. Look around your environment. Are there any witnesses who saw your abuser? Is there any CCTV at the location?

LOVE LETTERS / LETTERS OF APOLOGY

Many abusers will try and write letters and offer reasons why they have hurt you. Keep these letters safe and enter a record of these letters in your personal diary.

SEXUAL ASSAULT / RAPE

If this has happened to you then immediately ring the police. Do not clean any of your clothing or tidy up the area where the incident has occurred. Avoid bathing or showering, brushing your teeth, eating, drinking, smoking, consuming alcohol, taking medication, changing clothes, urinating, removing or inserting a tampon, wiping or cleaning the genital area.

You could attend a local Sexual Assault Referral Centre. The police will assist you in getting to this specialist place. You can refer yourself to such a centre.

4

**HOUSING
AND
CIVIL LAW**

Reproduced with kind permission by Stonewall Housing
Stonewall Housing
www.stonewallhousing.org
020 7359 5767 (advice)

Scenario 1 – I fear for my safety, I am in danger and I want to leave mypartner, I don't want my partner to find out where I am living. I need to get away in an emergency. **Go to page 44**

Scenario 2 - I have decided to leave my partner, and I am going to move out of my home, but I don't know what to do. Where can I go? What are my rights and entitlements? **Go to page 46**

Scenario 3 – I have moved out of our home, but my partner is pestering and threatening me. How can the law protect me? **Go to page 50**

Scenario 4 – I am staying at my home and my partner has left, what are my rights and entitlements? **Go to page 52**

Scenario 5 - I am staying at my home and my partner has begun to harass and pester me. What can I do? **Go to page 50** (SAME AS 3)

Scenario 6 – I have moved away from my partner and I need some support. **Go to page 57**

Scenario 7 - I have left my partner, but I need to go back to my home and collect my belongings? **Go to page 57**

ANSWER TO SCENARIO 1

GOING TO A REFUGE

A refuge is a safe house for people escaping domestic abuse. All women living in the refuge will have experienced domestic abuse and many survivors find it comforting moving into a place where people understand your problems. You can stay there for a night or for longer until you decide what you want to do in the long term. Most refuges issue licence agreements for six months but these can be extended should you need a longer time to sort out your housing needs.

The vast majority of refuges are for women. There are around 500 refuge organisations in the UK and about 70 in London. The addresses are confidential and not even known to the police. Safety is of paramount importance. Refuges use PO Box numbers instead of postal addresses, as these are harder to trace. The best thing about a refuge is that your abuser will not be able to find you unless you tell him/her where you are. If you are found by your abuser whilst you are living in the refuge, you will be asked to move into another refuge as remaining may put you and other people at risk. If you work, you may not be able to continue working from your previous work address. This is because your abuser may follow you, back to the refuge. The refuge address and the safety of you and the other residents is paramount.

There are some refuges that have self-contained family units but most refuges will usually give you your own room for yourself to share with your children. Other spaces - the living room, TV room, kitchen, playroom and possibly the bathroom - will be shared with other refuge residents. You will be expected to cook for yourself and your children. It is up to you and the other refuge residents whether or not you share cooking or eat together at mealtimes. You can be as self-contained or as sociable as you want to be.

Refuges employ support workers who can help you with your housing process and also offer emotional support. They sometimes also employ child support workers who can support your children whilst they adapt to life in a refuge. A refuge is a sanctuary where you can feel safe by moving away from abuse. Refuges remain the most useful and supportive environment to be able to make decisions about what you want to do next.

All refuges for women operate a women only policy. There is no age restriction on female children. With male children, refuges vary, with some only taking boys up to 12, whilst others take boys up to 18, (but only one boy over 14 at any one time). Women are expected to share bedrooms with their children. If you have children, they may have to change school, at least for a temporary period whilst you decide what you want to do. If there is a child support worker at the refuge, they will help you with this. Most refuges run playrooms, after schools clubs and go on organized trips out. The emphasis is on having fun, but also refuges are sensitive to the needs of children, who have witnessed and frequently experienced domestic abuse themselves. Many children enjoy living in a house where they can mix with other children. If you move to a refuge with your children, there will be lots of other children around for them to play with. Some children tell us that they miss their homes but enjoy living in a place where there is no violence and they are encouraged to have fun. There is an excellent website run by Women's Aid, designed for children who experience domestic violence at **www.thehideout.org.uk/**

You can call the Freephone National 24-hour Domestic Violence Helpline, which is run in partnership between Women's Aid and Refuge, and which will find a refuge space for you if you want this. In the case of men, refuge accommodation can be organized by ringing the Mankind helpline number **01823 334 244**

Prior to going to a refuge, gather all the essentials such as legal documents, house keys, identification, birth certificates, passports, documentation with your name on, benefit information, toiletries, children's toys, items of sentimental value etc. Disregard items that could easily identify you e.g. a personalized item of clothing etc.

ANSWER TO SCENARIO 2

STAYING WITH FRIENDS OR FAMILY

Staying with friends or family is only ever a short-term solution. It can be a helpful respite but it also has risks. Your friends or family may be very supportive and offer emergency accommodation and support at a time of crisis. This could give you the short-term space you need to make a decision about

what to do next.

This can be an unsuitable choice if your abuser knows the address. Your abuser may turn up at your friend or family member's address putting you and them at risk. Your friends or family may also try to convince you to reconcile with your abuser even if it is not safe for you to do so. They may even take your abuser's side. You should think carefully about whether this choice is right for you.

PRIVATE RENTING

The best thing about renting is that it's a quick way to move out of an abusive relationship into safe accommodation. The worst thing is that it can be expensive and offer limited security. If you have organised a viewing of a property, bring this book with you and make a list of the security features that you want amended. Ask the letting agent to comply with your requests, prior to signing any contracts.

Access to private rented accommodation depends on your budget. You will usually need to pay the landlord a month's rent in advance and a deposit equal to a month's rent. If you have the deposit and earn a low wage or claim benefits, including Job Seekers Allowance or Income Support, you may be entitled to claim Housing Benefit, which can help pay for your rent. However many landlords are reluctant to accept tenants who receive benefits. Councils have a cap on the contribution they will make through Housing Benefit. This means you will have to find cheaper properties. You may be able to find out more about the maximum level in your area by asking your local Citizens Advice Bureau. You can also fill out a pre- tenancy determination, which is a form you hand in to the council stating which property you intend to rent, that then lets you know the maximum level of Housing Benefit payable for that property. Some council housing departments run rent deposit schemes where tenants who wish to rent privately but who do not have a rent deposit, can ask the council to act as a bond to the landlord. If the tenant fails to pay his/her rent, the council promises to reimburse the landlord.

LOCAL AUTHORITY TEMPORARY ACCOMMODATION

Every borough has a local Housing Options and/or Homeless Persons Unit that can offer people housing advice and in some circumstances, emergency accommodation to people fleeing domestic abuse. This is interim accommodation whilst they make inquiries into your situation and decide if they have a duty to house you permanently.

If you have a joint tenancy, sometimes, with your agreement, the council or housing association will allow you to end the tenancy so that your partner has to leave, and may then grant you a new tenancy. It is very important that you get advice before taking this action, to ensure that you retain your housing rights. If you have a sole tenancy, it might be possible to approach your landlord and ask for a transfer into another property. You can do this either whilst you remain in the property, or move into temporary accommodation whilst a new property is found. The best thing about this option is that you do not risk becoming homeless. You retain your tenancy while you are negotiating a move into safe accommodation, and you do not have to accept accommodation that is not suitable. However, this option can take a lot of time to organise. If you would like a transfer you should contact your Housing Officer.

All council and housing association tenants are also able to apply for a mutual exchange, which involves swapping your home with another council or housing association tenant who wants to move. This option can be problematic in terms of your safety. If you exchange your tenancy with another tenant, the other tenant will know where you are living, and your safety will be in their hands should your abuser ask them for your new address. Unless you can arrange a three-way exchange, this option may not be safe.

If your landlord is the council or a housing association, you maybe able to get a transfer or a mutual exchange. Most local councils and housing associations have clear guidelines about dealing with tenants who are experiencing domestic abuse.

How do councils decide who gets housed?

The council has a legal duty to provide emergency accommodation to some people and if, after investigating your case, the council decides that you fulfil its criteria, it has a legal duty to help you find long-term accommodation. However the criteria are very stringent and not everyone will be able to get help from the council. The council considers five criteria when it decides whether to help you. These are:

- ❏ Are you eligible for assistance?
- ❏ Are you homeless?
- ❏ Are you in priority need?
- ❏ Are you intentionally homeless?
- ❏ Do you have a local connection?

Please read on for further information about what each of these criteria means.

4 Are you eligible for assistance?

The term eligibility relates to immigration status, and also to people who have spent a long time abroad and have recently returned to the UK. Eligibility is a complicated area and it is always worth getting advice. If you are currently claiming Job Seekers Allowance or Income Support, you are automatically eligible for assistance.

More information on European Union (EU) and European Economic Area (EEA) eligibility to housing is available from Shelter.

If you returned to the country recently or only came to the country for the first time recently (within the last six months), you may not be eligible for assistance, even if you are a UK citizen. In this situation, the council will decide whether you pass something called the **'Habitual Residence Test'**, which is a set of questions designed to find out if you are intending to remain in the UK as a resident and worker. The questions cover the length of time you have spent in the UK, why you came to the UK, what and where your long-term intentions are and where your centre of interest is, for example, if you have family or a business in the UK.

If you have the words 'no recourse to public funds' stamped on your passport, this may mean that you are ineligible, in which case, always check with advice line or a specialist immigration organisation as this area of law is very complex.

Are you homeless?

It is not considered reasonable for you to have to live in a home where you are at risk of violence, or threats of violence, which are likely to be carried out. This means that if you have experienced domestic abuse or threats of domestic abuse, the council should consider you to be homeless, even if you have a tenancy. It is worth bearing in mind that: You do not have to report the violence to the police You do not have to obtain a court order The abuser does not have to be the opposite sex Violence does not have to have taken place, for example threats of violence may be enough.

Are you in priority need?

Priority need is the term used to describe the way in which the council decides who to prioritise helping. Even if you are eligible and homeless, if you are not in priority need, the council will not offer you anywhere to stay. You are automatically in priority need if you:

- ❏ Have children who live with you
- ❏ Are pregnant
- ❏ Are under 18 years old and living on your own
- ❏ Are under 21 and were in 'care' for at least 13 weeks between the ages of from 16-18
- ❏ Are homeless as a result of an emergency, for example a flood or fire.

The council also has a duty to help people who are vulnerable. The definition of vulnerable which the council uses, is someone who is less likely to be able to fend for him or herself when homeless, so that they will suffer injury or detriment where a person who is not vulnerable would not experience this. This means, to be considered in priority need, you need to be more vulnerable then an average homeless person – having to sleep rough is not enough in itself. You may be considered to be at an additional risk of being vulnerable if you:

- ❏ Were a member of the armed forces.
- ❏ Have served a long prison sentence.
- ❏ Are an older person.
- ❏ Have a mental illness.
- ❏ Have a physical disability.
- ❏ Have another special reason to be considered vulnerable, or You have to leave your home because of violence (including domestic violence), or threats of violence, which are likely to be carried out.

Are you intentionally homeless?

People are considered to be intentionally homeless if they acted in a way, or failed to act in a way, which directly led to their homelessness. If you are fleeing your home as a result of domestic abuse, you will not be found intentionally homeless, even if you have rent arrears. The council may make inquiries about your previous addresses, especially if you have moved addresses recently. However they are not allowed, under any circumstances, to contact your abuser and question him/her about the reason you have left.

Do you have a local connection?

If you are experiencing domestic abuse, you can apply to any local council in the UK. You do not need a local connection. If you apply to your local area and tell the housing department you want to stay close to the area that your abuser lives, this may cause suspicion. If this is the case, you will need to state the reasons why you need to remain in your local area - for example, if you are caring for a relative or if your children have important exams and need to remain at school.

How do I apply?

If possible, get some advice before you go to the council. Go to any council housing department and, ideally, take an advice worker with you for support. Ask to see a homeless persons officer and tell them that you want to make an emergency housing application under part seven of the 1996 Housing Act. You may need to take a ticket and wait for your turn to be seen. You will be taken into a private cubicle and interviewed by a council worker. The council worker will ask you a series of questions about your current situation. If you are experiencing domestic abuse and you need to move as an emergency, you are entitled to be fully assessed. You will need to state clearly that it is an emergency and you have nowhere safe to return to that night. Do not be put off if you are told to return at a later date with more evidence. You are entitled to an assessment at this stage; you do not have to provide proof of abuse. If you meet the criteria and are deemed homeless, eligible for assistance and in priority need (see above), the council should place you into immediate interim accommodation while it investigates your case. This usually means a bed and breakfast (B&B) hotel. The B&B accommodation may not be in the area of your choice unless there is a good reason for you to be in a particular area - for example, you need to see a medical specialist very regularly or your children need to attend a specific school.

If the council has placed you in interim accommodation, it will then go on to make a full decision in your case. It should take no morethan 33 days. If it takes longer you should get advice. The council has a duty to tell you about any decision it makes, by giving you a 'section 184 letter'. If the council accepts a full duty to house you and you have children, you should not have to continue to live at the B&B for a more than six weeks. After six weeks, you should be moved into self-contained accommodation until you are permanently re- housed. If the council accepts a full duty to house you and you do not have children, you may have to continue to live at the B&B until you are permanently re-housed, unless you have a good reason to move into self- contained accommodation - for example, a significant medical reason. You will be sent a letter at this stage outlining the council's waiting list procedure or bidding scheme for permanent accommodation.

ANSWER TO SCENARIO 3

Whether or not you decide you want to leave your partner, you have a right to be protected under the law, and there are a number of legal options open to you, under both the criminal law and the civil law. The two systems are separate and are administered by separate courts:

❑   The **civil law** is primarily aimed at protection (or in some cases compensation.) A survivor of domestic violence can make an application for an injunction (a court order) either to the family proceedings court or the county court (usually through a solicitor).

❑   The **criminal law** is primarily aimed at punishing the offender. The police together with the Crown Prosecution Service (CPS) initiate the process. Criminal cases are heard in either the magistrates' court or the Crown Court depending on the severity of the charge.

If you claim benefits or have a low income, you may be entitled to help with legal costs via Legal Aid, now called Community Legal Services funding. The Community Legal Services website has information about applying for this funding, and there is a calculator enabling you to work out whether or not you are likely to be eligible. If you have a higher income, and are not entitled to funding, it is wise to ask the solicitor how much legal representation would cost before you engage them. If you are not in a position to pay for legal representation, it may be possible for you to put together your own case. If you are considering this, Rights of Women publish a domestic violence DIY injunction handbook. For more information go to www.rightsofwomen.org.uk

It is always best practice to seek legal advice.

It is important to get early advice. Your circumstances may change in a twenty four hour period. You could be applying for a civil injunction, whilst your abuser does an act that constitutes a criminal offence. Just because you are seeking protection from a civil court, doesn't mean that you cannot ring the police and ask for immediate protection. If your circumstances involve mixing the two processes. Make sure that the police and your solicitor understand what is actually going on. In some cases a lack of communication can halt progress. Everyone wants you to be safe.

You could try to gain some protection from your abuser by applying for a civil injunction. An injunction is a court order that requires someone to do or not to do something.

COURT UNDERTAKING

This is when the judge makes the abuser promise in court to stop his/her abusive behaviour. A breach of this is not a criminal offence.

NON-MOLESTATION ORDER

This is more serious. It will forbid the abuser from molesting you or your children, or damaging or throwing out your belongings. The term molestation includes physical, sexual and verbal abuse. The abuser does not need to have been violent. S/he could have been harassing you or intimidating you or your children. These orders may be given for a limited period of time. After they expire, you can apply again for another one.

How long does it take to get an injunction?

If you are in immediate danger, an application can be made to the court on the same day without your abuser being there. This is called a "without notice" or ex parte application. The court will need to consider whether or not you are at risk of significant harm, whether you will be prevented or deterred from applying if you have to wait, or whether your abuser is avoiding being served notice to appear before the court.

If the court grants a "without notice" order, you will have to return to court for a full hearing once your abuser has been served with notice.

If there are other family proceedings already in progress (e.g. for a residence or contact order for a child) the court may wish to hear the whole case together - but they can still grant an emergency order while you are waiting for the full hearing.

4 · What happens if the abuser breaks the order?

If your abuser breaks the terms of the injunction, and you are at all fearful for your safety or that of others, you should call the police. Under the Domestic Violence, Crime and Victims Act 2004, breach of a non-molestation injunction made on or after 1st July 2007 is a criminal offence. This means that the police should treat any breach of such an order just like any other criminal offence; so they should arrest your abuser, and take him/her to the magistrates' court, and not back to the county court or family proceedings court. This should strengthen the power of court orders.

HARASSMENT RESTRAINING ORDER / NON MOLESTATION ORDER

Both civil and criminal courts can issue this order. A judge can order any 'associated person' to stop harassing you. When related to restraining / non-molestation orders, an associated person includes a girlfriend or boyfriend, a casual sexual partner, stalkers and strangers. Harassment includes alarming, distressing and/or verbally insulting behaviour, on at least two occasions. Harassment is about a pattern of behaviour rather than one incident. It is therefore useful to keep a log of abusive behaviour. The civil courts can use the associated legal powers of the harassment act and they can issue a non-molestation order. The criminal courts use what is known as a restraining order. The difference is small. The evidence required for a criminal restraining order is greater than that of civil non-molestation.

To establish this for evidential purposes, the police usually issue a warning, so that it cannot later be claimed that s/he did not know their behaviour was distressing. Harassment is dealt with in a Magistrates court and carries a maximum sentence of six months imprisonment and/or a fine of up to £5000. Aggravated harassment, where a person threatens violence on at least two occasions, can be dealt with in either the Magistrates Court or Crown Court and carries a maximum sentence of five years and/or an unlimited fine. You may also be able to claim damages.

ANSWER TO SCENARIO 4

I am a registered civil partner with (or married to) my abuser

If you are registered civil partners or are married, you have additional housing rights whatever your tenancy type. The law says that as long as your partnership continues, you have occupation rights of the (family) home that you lived in as partners. This means that you can continue to live in your home, and your partner cannot change the locks or prevent your access, even if the home is in your partner's sole name. However, if the home is in your sole name, your partner will also have these rights, so you will need to take legal action to prevent your partner from being able to access your family home. You can do this by getting a civil order such as an occupation order.

Divorced and Dissolved?

If your partnership is dissolved or you are divorced, your rights may end, so it is very important that you get legal advice and take action to protect your long- term rights to your home.

We live together but are not civil partners or married

If you cohabit with your abuser, and are not registered civil partners or married, it is important that you get legal advice in order to find out all your rights and options concerning your home. If your home is in your name, or is in joint names with your abuser, you will have several options. If your home is solely in your abuser's name, you may have fewer options. You may need to go to court to get your rights recognised, and you can find more information about your options in the following sections.

EXCLUDED OCCUPIERS

An excluded occupier is someone who has very limited rights to remain in your home. Someone who lives with their landlord in their landlord's house is usually an excluded occupier. If either you or your abuser solely owns your home, or if the tenancy is in one of your sole names, the other may be an excluded occupier. If you are registered civil partners or a married couple, you will not be an excluded occupier until your partnership or marriage is dissolved or you are divorced.

An excluded occupier is only entitled to 'reasonable notice' to leave their home, and this notice does not have to be in writing. If you are the landlord and your abuser is the excluded occupier, this means that you may be able to give immediate notice as a result of the violence.

What are my housing rights if I decide to stay?

Once your abuser has left, you can change the locks. This is also the case for other relatives who aren't co-owners or co-tenants, should they become abusive. If you decide to change the locks, be aware that it is illegal to dispose of someone else's property. If your abuser returns to the property to collect his/her belongings, do not open the door unless there is a police escort with him/her. If your abuser is the sole owner or tenant, and you are the excluded occupier, you may be forced to leave at short notice. You should get a police escort to accompany you to collect your belongings.

My home is owned by me and/or my partner

If you are a sole owner and live with an abusive partner or family member, you may be able to change the locks and restrict your abuser from entering your home again.

If you are a joint owner, or you are registered civil partners, or married, or a cohabiting couple who share children, you may be able to obtain an occupation order. See the section called '**Occupation Order'** for more details. If your abuser is the sole owner, you may have fewer rights.

How do I stop my abuser from just selling my home?

If you are registered civil partners, or married, or joint owners of your home and you are concerned that your abuser is trying to sell your home without telling you, you may be able to prevent this. You can do this by registering an interest at the Land Registry. This is something you can do without the help of a solicitor and it protects your interests as your home cannot be sold or remortgaged without your consent. It is worth considering your abuser's potential reaction to you taking this action. When you register an interest in your home, your partner will be informed of that fact and may be very angry as this will cause complication, delay and legal expense for him/her at a sale. Think about your safety and plan this before taking any action.

What are my housing rights if I decide to stay?

If your abuser owns his/her home and you have lived there for some time and have contributed to the mortgage or the upkeep of the home, you may have some rights. If you are registered civil partners, or married, it may be easier to demonstrate these rights. If you are an unmarried co-habiting couple (of either sex), you may need to take legal advice if your home is in your partner's name only. You may have to take your partner to court to get your rights recognised. The courts will look at proof of bills in your name, all joint financial arrangements including joint bank accounts, proof of monies spent on (major) building improvements to your home and all receipts.

Evidence would also be needed if your partner deliberately tricked you into moving into his/her home and giving up your own home, with the intention of asking you to leave shortly after. Written contracts and evidence of verbal contracts will need to be presented in court before a decision can be made.

If you are not registered civil partners, or married, unless you made significant contributions to the cost of the home, or towards improvements to the home, you may be an excluded occupier (see the previous section for)

What if my partner solely owns our home?

If your tenancy is in your partner's name only, you may be an excluded occupier and have few rights. Again, check with the section on 'Excluded Occupiers' for more details. If you have children, you may have more rights and should seek further legal advice urgently. If you have a joint tenancy, you may apply to the civil court for an occupation order and also a tenancy transfer order into your sole name.

Demotion of tenancies

Most local authority or housing association tenants are issued with codes of behaviour. If the tenancy is in your sole or joint name and your abuser repeatedly causes a nuisance to neighbours or is destructive to your property, your housing association or local authority could attempt to demote your tenancy to an introductory tenancy in an attempt to force you to resolve your domestic situation.

If your abuser continues to cause a nuisance, you risk losing the tenancy altogether. To prevent a demotion of tenancy it may be useful to get civil protection from the court - for example, a nonmolestation order or an occupation order to prove to your landlords that you have taken steps to try and modify your abuser's behaviour.

My home is a housing co-op property

Housing co-ops have different types of tenancies to most rented accommodation and tenants are expected to contribute to running the co-op as well as maintaining their tenancy. If you live in a co-op, you should seek further legal advice to find out your rights.

My home is rented by me and/or my partner

My home is rented from a private landlord

If you live with your landlord or share a bathroom with your landlord or member of your landlord's family, you are likely to be an excluded occupier with very few housing rights. You should get legal advice by contacting Stonewall Housing's advice line as soon as possible. Most private landlords do not tolerate abusive behaviour that unsettles your neighbours or causes the destruction of their property. Most are happy to take steps to evict an abusive tenant and will co-operate with Sanctuary Schemes Some may try to evict you as well as your abuser. Your rights depend on the type of tenancy you have. Since February 1997, most private rented tenancies are Assured Shorthold Tenancies. If you started renting after that date and you were not given a written tenancy agreement, then this is the type of tenancy that you have. If your landlord attempts to evict you and or your abuser for noise nuisance or damage caused to the property and you have an Assured Shorthold Tenancy, s/he will need to issue you with two months written notice, that cannot expire before the last day of the first six month period. You will have no grounds to oppose this eviction. If you do not move out when the written notice expires, your landlord will have to obtain a possession order and then an eviction order before you have to leave. This may take some months to obtain. Once s/he has obtained these, a bailiff will be sent to your home to evict you. In this situation, you may have to pay court fees. Private tenancies issued before February 1997 may have significantly increased rights and it may be much more difficult for your landlord to evict you. It is very important that you seek advice if you think this may apply to you. You may also be entitled to apply for a court order that could prevent your abuser from accessing your home. Civil orders are not available to you if you have an Assured Shorthold Tenancy.

OCCUPATION ORDER

This type of order can be used to decide what should happen to your home. Depending on the circumstances, an occupation order might be used to:

❑ Force your abuser to leave your home

- ❑ Force your abuser to remain a certain distance away from your home
- ❑ Force your abuser to keep away from a specified part of your home
- ❑ Force your abuser to give you access to your home, if for example s/he has forced you out and changed the locks.

The type of occupation order you may be able to apply for will depend on whether you are an 'entitled' or a 'non-entitled' person. Entitlement is about whether you have a legal right to remain in your home.

ENTITLED PEOPLE

An entitled person usually has property rights in their own name - for example, as a joint tenant or owner. Alternatively, if you are a married or registered civil partner of your abuser, but not a joint tenant or owner, you will still be an 'entitled person'. The judge will look at both sides' housing needs, finances, investments, safety issues, the conduct of the people involved, and the welfare of any children involved.

Occupation orders for entitled people can last indefinitely or for a specified period of time, depending on what the judge decides.

NON-ENTITLED PEOPLE

You are a non-entitled person if you cohabit with your partner and do not have property rights in your own name. However, even as a non-entitled person, you may still the have right to obtain a lesser type of occupation order. The judge will look at both sides' housing needs, finances, investments, safety issues, the conduct of the people involved, and the welfare of any children involved. The judge will also consider the nature of your relationship, how long you have lived together as partners and/or how long you have lived apart, if there are or have been any children [involved], and if there are any other issues relating to the transfer of property or assets.

Occupation orders for non-entitled people can last for six months, with the possibility of extending it for a further six months. After a maximum of one year, an abuser can return to his/her home.

What types of court order are there?

TRANSFER OF TENANCY ORDER

The judge can order your abuser to sign over his/her secure or assured tenancy. Abusive people who were or are part of a cohabiting couple, married or civil partners, risk losing their tenancy even if it is held in their sole name. To qualify for this, both partners must have lived in the home together as if husband and wife or as if civil partners. If you have never lived at the address where the tenancy is held, you cannot apply for this order. To decide who gets the tenancy, the judge will look at the circumstances when the tenancy was first granted, whether you or your abuser is a suitable tenant, the housing needs and resources available to both of you and, where applicable, your children, and the health and well-being of both parties and any children. Where couples are cohabiting and the sole tenancy is held by your abuser, the judge will also consider the nature of the relationship, its duration, if you have children, and where applicable, the length of time which has elapsed since separating.

ANSWER TO SCENARIO 6

FURTHER SUPPORT

How do I protect my new address?

If you move into new accommodation and you suspect that your abuser will try to find you, you can arrange to have your mail redirected to a secure PO Box address. The local post office will be able to help you with this. If you return to your old area, make sure you are not followed to your new address. This may seem a bit paranoid but if you make the effort to move to safety, the worst thing would be to be found as this may force you to move again to keep safe.

How will I afford new furniture?

If you move to a new place and cannot afford any new furniture, there are a number of options. If you have been claiming Job Seekers Allowance or Income Support for at least 26 weeks, you may be entitled to a Community Care Grant or a Budgeting Loan from the Department of Work and Pensions to help you with these costs. A number of organisations exist which sell second-hand furniture to homeless people at low costs, and these may be available in your area. It may also be possible to make applications to local charities, which support people in their local area who are experiencing hardship.

ANSWER TO SCENARIO 7

POLICE ASSISTANCE

What is a police escort?

The police offer people escaping domestic abuse an escort back to their home to protect them while they retrieve their belongings. This is to prevent a breach of the peace. As this is usually not a police priority, it is best to approach the nearest police station to your home early in the morning when they are less busy. You can arrange for this to happen by phoning in advance and speaking to a Duty Sergeant on the front desk. The police will accompany you to your home. They will intervene if your abuser tries to prevent you from taking your belongings. The police will not

4 help you carry your belongings out of your home. They will make sure you leave the area without being followed. It is illegal for anyone to withhold your passport or belongings. If you arrive and find that your abuser had hidden your belongings, a court order can be obtained to force him or her to hand these over.

CHAPTER SUMMARY

- ❑ *If you are living in fear, you can leave your home at anytime and stay at a UK refuge.*
- ❑ *Seek advice from a solicitor at the earliest opportunity.*
- ❑ *Seek advice from a housing officer at the earliest opportunity.*
- ❑ *Prepare a housing statement.*
- ❑ *Contact the police if you need to return to your previous address.*

5

**CHILD
CONTACT**

5 Child contact

Child Contact is not an easy issue and a number of issues need to be considered. This chapter is designed to make you think about the various options available to you. If your ex-partner has been previously violent, acted with great control and displayed resentment / jealousy in the past, you will have to re-evaluate your personal safety and legal options. If however your partner hasn't been particularly violent, the threat of controlled access, may put you in danger. It is best to approach this issue with caution.

If you are considering not involving a legal process, from the very start both of you have to agree a practical child care plan. Within an agreed plan, you must consider two practicalities: Personal Safety and the social and emotional needs of your children. Emotions such as anger and jealousy on both sides can quickly change this process and may make the situation volatile and un-predictable. Many ex-partners can become particularly abusive when a new partner or friend enters your life. Ex-partners show hostility when it comes to parenting decisions. If you haven't a legal agreement, some ex-partners come and go as they please and make excuses for turning up at your home address. These excuses can be misconstrued "I was missing the kids""I forgot to give the children something". It may be that your ex-partner is actually keeping a watchful eye over you, in essence you are being stalked. In order to avoid confrontational situations, you must set and agree boundaries, for example:

❑ You are not to come to my home, unless I contact you first.

❑ If you make more than x phone calls a day, I will consider this to be harassment.

❑ There will be no surprise visits.

❑ The day that we meet, I will drop the children to your mother's home (or a friend's home).

❑ You must return at a set time, if you're going to be late, please contact me at your earliest convenience.

❑ I will pick the children up from school and I have informed the school about this arrangement.

If however your approach isn't working, remember to add this in your domestic violence diary. It may be a good time to contact a solicitor. It is very important for you to have a really good - sympathetic and experienced - solicitor.

Your solicitor will discuss your relationship and will then write a statement concerning your experiences, needs and concerns. The solicitor will apply to the court for a court hearing. This (you will be notified) will take place in a civil or county court.

ON THE COURT DAY

Before you leave, remember to bring with you your domestic abuse diary. If you can, dress in a sensible and business-like way, and ask your solicitor or the court Usher (the person who tells you to go into the court rooms) what to call the judges. In a Magistrates Court it is usually Sir or Madam. In other courts it may be Your Honour or Your Lordship/Ladyship.

When the Judge or Magistrates arrive, everyone stands up. Watch for what the court people do. Sit down when they do. There will be more standing up when the magistrates leave the court room.

When a solicitor asks a question, pause, think about the answer and turn to face the judge and answer slowly.

PERSONAL SAFETY

The actual weekly exchange of your children can be stressful and may involve incidents of derogatory behavior, what ever is said consider your safety and how you gather evidence.

Children can sometimes unwittingly, reduce your personal safety, for example: Opening the door to your ex-partner, once the abuser is in side your property your safety can be compromised. The opportunities for help also reduce.

If you are going to arrange contact, arrange handover in an open space, where there are lots of people around and where there is council cctv. If you can bring a witness and make sure you have your mobile phone with you. Re-visit the previous chapter "Personal Safety"

CAFCASS STANDS FOR CHILDREN AND FAMILY COURT ADVISORY SUPPORT SERVICE.

Cafcass is independent of the courts, social services, education and health authorities and all similar agencies.

What does Cafcass do?

Cafcass safeguards and promotes the welfare of children involved in family court proceedings. It advises the court so that the decisions it makes are in the best interests of children. Cafcass only works in the family courts. These are not criminal courts. When parents or carers separate they can usually agree about the arrangements for their children. However, if they can't, one of them may make an application to the court for the court to decide about those arrangements. If that happens the court will usually ask a Children and Family Reporter from Cafcass to help.

5 The Welfare Checklist - section 1 Children Act 1989

When a Court considers any question relating to the upbringing of the child under the Children Act 1989 the court must have regard to the welfare checklist set out in s1 of that Act. Among the things the court must consider are:

❑ The ascertainable wishes and feelings of the child concerned (considered in light of his age and understanding);

❑ His physical, emotional and/or educational needs;

❑ The likely effect on him of any change in his circumstances;

❑ His age, sex, background and any characteristics of his, which the court considers relevant;

❑ Any harm which he has suffered or is at risk of suffering;

❑ How capable each of his parents and any other person in relation to whom the court considers the question to be relevant, is of meeting his needs;

❑ The range of powers available to the court under the Children Act 1989 in the proceedings in question.

For all proceedings under the Children Act 1989 when the court considers a question of the child's upbringing the child's welfare is the court's paramount consideration.

Parental Responsibility - sections 3 and 4 Children Act 1989

Parental responsibility means all the rights, duties, powers, responsibilities and authority, which by law a parent of a child has in relation to the child and his property.

The birth mother of a child will always have parental responsibility unless it is extinguished by the making of an adoption order to another person.

Where the child's father and mother are married to each other at the time of the birth, they both have parental responsibility for the child.

Where the child's mother and father are not married to each other at the time of the birth the general rule is that the mother has sole parental responsibility for the child. However, if a child's birth is registered or re-registered from 1 December 2003 and the unmarried father is named on the Register, this also gives him parental responsibility.

Other ways in which a father can obtain parental responsibility are by:

❑ drawing up an agreement with the mother (a parental responsibility agreement), which is a specific form that has to be signed by both parents and lodged with the court;

- ❏ marrying the mother; or

- ❏ the court making a parental responsibility order if the parents cannot agree on the father having parental responsibility.

More than one person can have parental responsibility for the same child at the same time. Parental responsibility is shared between everyone, but individuals can act alone and without the others in meeting responsibilities to safeguard and protect the child.

Residence Orders - section 8 Children Act 1989

These orders decide where the child is to live and with whom. The granting of a residence order to someone automatically gives him or her parental responsibility for the child if they do not already have it. Parental responsibility obtained as a result of a residence order will continue until the order ceases.

A residence order lasts until the child is 16 unless the circumstances of the case are exceptional and the court has ordered that it continue for longer.

A residence order can be granted to more than one person and can be made jointly to an unmarried couple.

A residence order prevents anyone changing the surname of or removing from the UK (for more than 1 month) any child who is the subject of the order without the agreement of everyone with parental responsibility or an order of the court.

Contact Orders - section 8 Children Act 1989

These are orders that require the person with whom a child lives to allow that child to visit, stay or have contact with a person named in the order.

Orders continue until the child is 16 years. The court will only make contact orders for children over 16 years old in exceptional circumstances.

Contact can either be direct e.g. face-to-face meetings with a person or indirect e.g. by letter, video, exchange of Christmas cards etc.

Some orders will be very specific as to times, dates and arrangements for contact, other orders will be more open with detailed arrangements to be made between the parties by agreement.

These orders are not just obtained by parents for contact with their children, there can also be orders for contact between siblings or the child and wider family members.

Sometimes the order will give directions that the contact is to be supervised by a third person. The order may also only be for a specific period or contain provisions which operate for a specific period.

These are orders of the court and to not comply with them can be a contempt of court with serious consequences.

What are Children and Family Reporters?

Children and Family Reporters are officers of Cafcass and they are independent of the courts, social services, education and health authorities and all similar agencies. They are qualified in social work and experienced in working with children and families. The welfare of children is always their chief concern.

Every family is different, and Children and Family Reporters will follow the course of action most appropriate to your specific circumstances.

In general, Children and Family Reporters are asked to help families agree sensible arrangements for their children. This is usually when parents have not managed to do that themselves, or with the help of solicitors or mediators (mediators are available from when you split up to help you reach agreement). All courts want families to sort things out themselves as much as possible, and everyone involved with the court will try to help families work out the best possible arrangements for the children. When a parent or carer applies to court, the court will sometimes ask a Children and Family Reporter to meet with them and the other parent or adults to see if things can be sorted out without having to go on with the court case. If no agreement is reached, the Children and Family Reporter may be asked to write a report for the court, which explains the enquiries they have made and says what they think should happen. The court will decide whether to order a report.

What happens when I first go to court?

Different courts operate in different ways across England and Wales. It is likely that you will see a judge or magistrate who will want to find out the issues for the children. If there is a Children and Family Reporter at court, the judge or magistrate may ask them to meet with you and the other parent. They will want to see:

❑ What you can agree

❑ What you can't agree

❑ Whether there are any areas the court needs to look into such as violence or risk to the children.

If matters can be agreed and there are no serious issues to be investigated, the court may be able to end the process at that stage, either by making agreed court orders or no orders being necessary.

If there is still no agreement between the parents, the Children and Family Reporter can then advise the court what should happen next. This could be:

- Spending more time away from court with a mediator or Children and Family Reporter to help reach agreement

- The court hearing being adjourned so that the Children and Family Reporter can write a full welfare report on all the children's circumstances

- Other enquiries on specific issues such as health

- A hearing for the judge or magistrates to decide what orders, if any, should be made.

What are welfare reports?

The court often asks the Children and Family Reporter to write a report about what he or she thinks is best for the child. This usually takes about ten weeks. It is still quite common for agreement to be reached during this time. When the report is finished, it goes to the court. It is also sent to your solicitor if you have one, or direct to you if you don't so that you know what is being said in the report before the court hearing. The report is confidential and must not be shown to anyone else.

What will the Children and Family Reporter talk about with my child?

The Children and Family Reporter will especially want to meet and talk with your child. In order to decide what is best for a child the court needs to know about your child's wishes and feelings. It is a very important part of the role of the Children and Family Reporter to tell the court what these are.

The Children and Family Reporter will not ask your children to take sides or ask which parent they like best. Instead the Children and Family Reporter will talk with your children about how they can best stay close to both parents – practical things like school and who does what in the family.

Who else will the Children and Family Reporter talk to for the report?

As well as talking with your child, with you and with the other parent, the Children and Family Reporter often needs to talk to other people who can provide information about you or your child. For example, they may need to talk to your doctor, teachers, relatives, health visitors and social workers. The court may ask the Children and Family Reporter to speak to a particular person. These enquiries will be confidential to the family proceedings, unless any information is given that a child is at risk. You will also see what is being said when you read the report. The Children and Family Reporter will let you know who they are talking to and will ask for your agreement when they need to. It is normal to make enquiries of the police, social services (including the child protection register) and to see information already held by Cafcass.

Will I have to see the other parent or adult involved?

No, not if you don't want to. A joint meeting may be suggested, but you have the right to be seen on your own, especially if you are afraid of the other parent.

Is what I tell the Children and Family Reporter confidential?

What is said to the Children and Family Reporter may be used in the report that is given to the court. All information remains confidential to the court, the parties to the case, and other people involved in the report process. The Children and Family Reporter cannot give information to anyone else without the permission of the court. However, the Children and Family Reporter must tell the court any information that is relevant to the welfare of your child. They could contact the Local Authority or the police child protection unit if a child is at risk. This does not happen often but it is important that you know this could happen.

Will the court do what my child wants?

Not necessarily. The court has to act in what it considers to be the best interests of your child. However, in doing this the wishes and feelings of your child will be considered, taking into account their age and level of understanding.

Will the court always do what the Children and Family Reporter advises?

It is the court that decides what will happen, but the court will take careful notice of what the Children and Family Reporter says. If a court disagrees with what a Children and Family Reporter has recommended it will explain why.

What if I'm not happy with what the Children and Family Reporter is doing or what is in the report?

While the report is being prepared, you should let the Children and Family Reporter know if you are unhappy. If it can't be resolved, talk to your solicitor or to your local Cafcass manager. If you disagree with the contents of the report you or your solicitor need to raise this at a court hearing. You can ask the court to order the Children and Family Reporter to attend court and answer questions about his/her enquiries and report contents. It is very important that you do tell the court if you are unhappy with anything in the report, as it is harder to put it right later once the court proceedings are finished.

Which parent will the Children and Family Reporter favour?

The Children and Family Reporter will favour neither parent. They are impartial and always treat the welfare of the children as their main priority. The Children and Family Reporter will speak to many different people and look at your family's particular set of circumstances. They will make their recommendations based on this information.

6

FINANCIAL SUPPORT

6 Financial Support

After you have left an abusive relationship you may experience one of two emotions. You may feel joyous, it is now an opportunity for you to make financial decisions, without being criticised, emotionally blackmailed or threatened. You may be feeling apprehensive about having full financial control. The financial aspect of your life can be confusing, there are so many companies that boast financial help, but actually want to take more money than is required. Be cautious about your finances, financial companies offer some attractive solutions but rarely offer the personal support and advice that is needed. Loan sharks operate across the UK.

There is one financial authority who seeks to protect, educate and inform. www. moneysavingexpert.com is the website that has helped millions of people across the UK. Martin Lewis is trusted, ethical and honest. The website has many benefits to the user. Martin advises to budget correctly and his website provides a free tool to help you consider where you are with your finances. Martin advises you to:

Cut household bills

Gas and Electricity, Food Shopping, Council Tax, Home Phone & Broadband, Childcare costs, Cut boiler cover costs, Free international calls, Water Meters, Sky & Virgin Media TV Cost Cutting, Direct Debit, Existing credit card debts, Mortgages, Existing loans, Cheaper Prescriptions & Medications, Train Fares, Petrol.

Cut personal bills

Car Insurance, Home Insurance, Roadside Assistance, Life Insurance and Mortgage Payment Protection Insurance .

Increase access to extra money

- ❏ Benefit Check-up and Pension Boosting

- ❏ Mortgage Arrears Help

- ❏ Grants that you are entitled too

- ❏ Childcare Tax Credits

In terms of benefits the website **Entitledto.co.uk** does the work for you: it has a regularly updated calculator that works everything out. It's very simple to use: just input basic details about your personal situation, such as income, council tax bill, and your savings and it reveals what, if any, benefits you're entitled to.

The calculator includes all the main benefits: Working Tax Credit; Council Tax and Housing Benefit; Pension Credit; Child Benefit; Child Trust Fund and Child Tax Credit. It's important to remember, benefits rules do change, so if it's likely you're entitled to benefits then it's worth doing an annual check up.

Local Councils also offer the same service and have a viable benefits service.

Other sources of finance include maintenance payments. Martin Lewis actively supports families by listing nationwide freebees. This includes cheap days out for all persons, shopping vouchers, supermarket coupons and other free offers. These types of offers could serve to promote your health and well being.

Other ways to save

Car-boot sales / charity shops provide a cheap way of acquiring nearly new items; it is amazing what people are selling on a daily basis at very reasonable prices. Government and police auctions also provide a very cost effective way of acquiring nearly new goods. The website **www.freecycle.org** is a new concept where people can exchange items for free. Simply post a wanted or offered description and see what happens.

Good money saving books

- ❏ The Money Diet: The Ultimate Guide to Shedding Pounds Off Your Bills and Saving Money on Everything! (Paperback) By (author) Martin Lewis

- ❏ Mr Thrifty's How to Save Money on Absolutely Everything (Paperback) By (author) Jane Furnival

- ❏ How I Lived a Year on Just a Pound a Day (Paperback) By (author) Kath Kelly

Charities can also help with items of household furniture.

Emmaus shops (**www.emmaus.org.uk**)sell a wide range of good quality items at great prices: second-hand furniture, household goods and much more. From sofas to sewing machines, books to bicycles, you never know what you might find. Some items will have been refurbished in the Emmaus workshops; some shops also sell new items made in the workshops, such as garden furniture from reclaimed wood, bird boxes, even stained glass! Emmaus offer discounts to people who can prove that they are on benefits or that times are tough.

Benefits

The benefits system provides practical help and financial support if you are unemployed and looking for work. It also provides you with additional income when your earnings are low, if you are bringing up children, are retired, care for someone, are ill or have a disability.

Who pays benefits?

The Department for Work and Pensions (DWP) manages most benefits through Job centre Plus offices. Benefits and entitlements for pensioners are dealt with through a network of pension centre's which provide a face-to-face service for those who need additional help and support. You'll also often deal with other agencies or government departments, such as your local council or HM Revenue & Customs (HMRC).

Child Benefit is a tax-free payment that you can claim for your child. It is usually paid every four weeks but in some cases can be paid weekly, and there are separate rates for each child. The payment can be claimed by anyone who qualifies, whatever their income or savings. The only way to claim Child Benefit is to fill in a Child Benefit claim form and send it to the Child Benefit Office along with your child's birth or adoption certificate. You can't claim over the phone or the internet.

If you have problems getting a claim form, and are calling from the UK, please contact the Child Benefit Helpline on 0845 302 1444 or text phone 0845 302 1474.

Tax credits are payments from the government. If you're responsible for at least one child or young person who normally lives with you, you may qualify for Child Tax Credit. If you work, but earn low wages, you may qualify for Working Tax Credit. To claim tax credits you have to fill in a claim form. You can order a tax credits claim pack from the Tax Credit Helpline on 0845 300 3900 or text phone 0845 300 3909.

Council Tax

If you need financial help to pay your Council Tax bill, you may be able to get Council Tax Benefit. You may also get Second Adult Rebate if you share your home with another adult (not your partner or civil partner) who's unable to pay towards the Council Tax.

Child Maintenance can make an important difference to a child's well-being. The parent without the main day-to-day care of the child pays child maintenance to the other parent to help toward the child's everyday living costs. Find out more about your child maintenance options.

Your child maintenance options

If you are a parent it is important that your financial responsibility for your child does not end if your relationship with the other parent ends. Putting an effective child maintenance agreement in place can make a notable difference to a child's well-being.

The two main options you can choose from for arranging a child maintenance agreement are:

❑ making a private arrangement with the other parent

❑ using the Child Support Agency (CSA) as the statutory maintenance service to calculate and collect maintenance for you

The following benefits are claimed at your local job center plus To make a claim for benefit - call 0800 055 6688 (8am - 6pm Monday to Friday). A text phone service is available if you have a speech or hearing impairment 0800 023 4888. **www.jobcentreplus.gov.uk**

Community Care Grant

If you need financial help to live independently in the community or to ease exceptional pressure on you and your family you may be able to get a Community Care Grant. You don't have to pay it back.

Income Support benefit

If you can't be available for full-time work and don't have enough money to live on, you may be able to get Income Support benefit. Whether you qualify or not and how much you get depends on your circumstances.

Housing Benefit

If you're on a low income and need financial help to pay all or part of your rent, you may be able to get Housing Benefit. You may get Housing Benefit if you pay rent and your income and capital (savings and investments) are below a certain level. If you rent from a private landlord you may qualify for Local Housing Allowance, if you are making a new claim for Housing Benefit or moving address.

Disability Living Allowance

Disability Living Allowance - sometimes referred to as DLA - is a tax-free benefit for children and adults who need help with personal care or have walking difficulties because they are physically or mentally disabled.

Jobseeker's Allowance

Jobseeker's Allowance is the main benefit for people of working age who are out of work or work less than 16 hours a week on average. If you're eligible, it is paid while you're looking for work.

Crisis Loan

If you need financial help with an emergency or disaster you may be able to get a Crisis Loan; the interest-free loan from the Social Fund that you pay back.

Warm Front Scheme in England

If you need help paying for heating and insulation improvements in your privately owned or rented home, you, your partner or civil partner may be able to get money from the government's Warm Front grants scheme if, for example, you're receiving income or disability-related benefits

Hospital Travel Costs Scheme

You may be able to get financial help from the Hospital Travel Costs Scheme if you're on a low income, need NHS treatment at a hospital, other NHS centre or private clinic and have been referred by an NHS hospital consultant.

Most National Health Service (NHS) treatment is free but there can be charges for some things. You may be able to get help with NHS health costs if for example you're on a low income.

Healthy Start scheme

You may be entitled to free milk, fresh fruit and vegetables, infant formula and vitamins under the Healthy Start scheme.

Statutory Sick Pay

If you're an employee and unable to work because you're ill you may be able to get Statutory Sick Pay. It is paid by your employer and can be paid for up to 28 weeks.

Community Legal Advice

You may be able to get free legal help if you can't afford it. Community Legal Advice offers this service through legal advisers and solicitors, specialist advice agencies and other public organisations.

www.communitylegaladvice.org.uk/

Debt Problems

National Debtline is a national telephone helpline for people with debt problems in England, Scotland and Wales. The service is free, confidential and independent. The service was set up in 1987. National Debtline is part of the Money Advice Trust, (registered charity no 1099506). The service provides self-help advice to its callers and also produces written self-help packs and factsheets to back this up. The service can also assist callers with the setting up of Debt Management Plans for England & Wales, Debt Relief Orders for England & Wales or Debt Management Plans for Scotland.

FREEPHONE: 0808 808 4000

Monday to Friday 9am to 9pm

Saturday 9.30am to 1pm

www.nationaldebtline.co.uk

CHAPTER SUMMARY

6

- ❑ *Prepare a budget plan.*
- ❑ *Apply for all entitled benefits.*
- ❑ *Visit your local car boot sale or charity shop.*
- ❑ *Access help for your debts.*
- ❑ *Be cautious with your finances, if it seems too good to be true, it probably is.*

7

**THE
CRIMINAL
JUSTICE
SYSTEM**

THE POLICE

The police are a key 24 hour agency for people who are experiencing domestic abuse. They should be the first people you call for in an emergency. The police have a number of short to long term practical solutions that can help your distressing set of circumstances.

If you call 999 the police will attend as quickly as possible and can offer the following interventions:

Short term – They can arrest and take away the abuser using a number of police powers. This ensures that you are safe from harm and that you get some time to relax and consider your needs and options available to you. The police may arrange for first aid or medical treatment.

Medium term – The police will ask you a number of questions and will risk assess your current living arrangements. This will ensure that a care plan is followed up and other agencies are aware of your household issues. You may be referred to other agencies who can support you. For example women's aid, housing, social services, drug and alcohol services, etc.

Long term – The police can help, support and investigate an allegation of wrong doing. For example if you have been assaulted, harassed or raped. The police are the first agency within the criminal justice system and will guide you from reporting a crime to the actual conviction of the abuser. The role of the police is to investigate crime and secure the necessary evidence. The police can also advise you with regard to your personal safety. A crime prevention officer can be called upon to install panic alarms and secure your home correctly. If you are concerned about your personal safety and would like to be referred to a crime prevention officer please ask this to be recorded on the police risk assessment form. *NB* service standards vary across the UK.

The legal system explained simply

The Legal System can be compared to making a special film. The writers of the film's script are lawyers and judges. They decide what script will be used, and they write the law. You are an actor in the film, but you can alter the film's story. You have been involved in an incident and you contact the police. The police act as the film makers, and have a film crew, director and many assistants. They record what you have to say, they organise make-up artists and runners. The police take photos of what has happened. They contact other actors and record what they have got to say. They also interview the person who has abused you and record what he or she has got to say.

The police make your film and present it to a Crown Prosecution Service (CPS) solicitor. The CPS solicitor edits the film and will decide if the film is of a good standard. The CPS decides whether the film can be released to the general public and then release it to the courts. The CPS, not the police, decides to prosecute the abuser. The courts receive the film and the person abusing you has an opportunity to say if the film was recorded correctly and that they have been abusing you. If the person abusing you decides not to admit that the film was correctly made he/she can then ask the court to play the making of the film. The court watches the making of the film and then decides if the person abusing you has acted against the law. The judge or magistrate in the court then punishes the abuser for breaking the law.

Criminal Law

The criminal law is used by many different agencies not just the police. This type of law is administered in a Magistrate's Court and Crown Court. Less serious offences are dealt with in the Magistrate's Court. The legal system requires a hefty weight of evidence and a case has to be proved beyond reasonable doubt.

UK LAW

There is not a UK law that protects you against domestic violence specifically. However, there are many laws that can be used depending on what has happened to you.

- ❑ Common Assault
- ❑ Actual Bodily Harm
- ❑ Grievous Bodily Harm without intent
- ❑ Grievous Bodily Harm with intent
- ❑ Domestic Burglary
- ❑ Harassment

Miscellaneous Offences (Criminal Law)

- ❑ Blackmail
- ❑ Kidnap
- ❑ Racially aggravated offences
- ❑ Using violence to secure entry into premises
- ❑ Sexual offences
- ❑ Public order offences

When the police arrive

Tell the police officers what has exactly happened and how you feel. Explain to them the types of abuse that you have been exposed to. Tell the police that you want to be safe and want the abuser to be taken away. Answer all questions as honestly as possible. It may make the difference to the type of risk assessment that is carried out.

The police officers who have attended may ask you the following questions:

- ❑ Do you want to make a complaint against the abuser?
- ❑ Do you want to press charges against the abuser?
- ❑ Are you willing to attend court?

These types of questions are not supportive and do not explain clearly the ongoing support and care that you will receive. The word complaint is misunderstood.

By making a **statement** you are asking the police officer to listen and record what type of mistreatment you have suffered. You are asking the officer to seize and preserve evidence of a crime. You are asking the officer to be supportive from the very beginning, allowing the officer to liaise with other specialists who can and will support you. You are admitting that your relationship is not healthy and asking for help.

And lastly you are asking the officer to support you in the event of a court case. Not all cases get to court. Making a statement to the police ensures that you are guided along the paths of people who understand you and wish to help you. It is not as daunting as you will first think.

MAKING A STATEMENT TO THE POLICE

The police will ask you a number of questions and draft a rough statement. They will then clarify and delve deeper into what has happened. It is at this stage a statement will be written. It is important to understand that it is your statement and it should be written in your own language.

You may have to be video interviewed. This is a procedure that provides the police with the best possible evidence. This evidence can be played to the Court. Tell the police exactly what happened, including what you saw and heard. Tell them if you fear for your, or your family's safety. Tell them if the crime was made worse by abuse related to race, sexuality, religion or disability.

Whilst at your home the police may take photographs, arrange an appointment with your GP or even take you to hospital. After the evidential statement has been taken, you will be asked to provide a Victim Personal Statement.

MAKING A VICTIM PERSONAL STATEMENT

A Victim Personal Statement (VPS) is a written account of how you feel and how the abuse has affected you. The VPS will be used after the abuser has been convicted in a court of law. After a traumatic event has taken place it can be very difficult to put into words how the trauma has affected you. It may be some time before you can clearly express yourself. Don't worry, you can add to your statement at a later time. Here are some guidelines that you might like to think about:

- ❑ How has the crime affected your life?
- ❑ Bail – Do you have any concerns about the suspect being bailed?
- ❑ Information – How often would you like to be updated?
- ❑ Concerns – What concerns do you have about the court process?
- ❑ Are you going to claim compensation?
- ❑ Would you like the police to apply for a Restraining Order if your abuser is convicted at court?
- ❑ Has your behaviour changed because you have been abused?
- ❑ Socialising – Do you see friends and relatives less?
- ❑ Children – How has the abuse affected your children?
- ❑ Self Esteem – Do you feel trapped and less confident?
- ❑ Relationships – Are you more pessimistic about a future relationship?
- ❑ Future - Are you nervous about the future?
- ❑ Feelings – Are you suffering from panic attacks or anxiety?
- ❑ **Restraining Order - If you are still concerned about your personal safety ask the police to apply for a restraining order on conviction.**

SPECIAL MEASURES

The witness service and police will support you. If you are a vulnerable witness the police will assess this prior or during your interview statement. What this means is that the police and CPS will be able to apply to the court for special measures. Special measures are instructions that allow the court to become more people friendly.

For instance a victim can request the following:

- ❑ Physically placing a screening between the witness and the abuser in Crown Court.
- ❑ Evidence from the witness by live link (via a video camera) in Crown Court and Magistrates' Courts. You won't have to enter court and you won't see your abuser.
- ❑ Evidence given in private in Crown Court and Magistrates' Courts.
- ❑ Removal of wigs and gowns in court (not applicable for magistrates).
- ❑ The use of video recorded evidence in court paints a true picture.

How do I strengthen my case?

In order for you to be successful in court you have to give as much detail as you possibly can, and don't leave anything out. If you have been dishonest tell the police in the first instance. If you omit something from your statement you will undermine your case. Be honest. Never take matters into your own hands, as you will weaken your case and jeopardise your chances of a successful outcome.

What should I do after I have given a statement?

After you have given your statement, it may be a good time to speak to a person who understands your experiences, supports your needs and can arrange further support. It's only a phone call - please make that call. You are not alone.

What is an arrest?

An arrest is the use of a legal power to force the abuser to be detained at a designated police station. The reasoning for an arrest may be due to a number of factors, these include:

Preventing serious further harm being caused; investigating an allegation of a crime or preventing further crimes being committed against you.

What happens to the abuser at the police station?

The abuser will be well treated and looked after. Firstly a risk assessment will be carried out ensuring that the police understand the abuser's needs. If the abuser requires medical treatment or medication then these needs will be met. The abuser will be given an opportunity to sober up from either the influence of alcohol or drugs. The abuser has the following rights:

- ❑ The right to speak to a duty solicitor.

- ❑ The right to inform someone that they are being detained at the police station. They will not contact you.

- ❑ The right to read the codes of practice detailing the way in which the police should treat them.

Once the officer in the case (OIC) has thoroughly investigated the circumstances of the crime he or she will then interview the abuser. This will give the abuser an opportunity to give their side of the story.

The police have strictly limited powers as to the length of time they can keep an abuser at the police station (usually 24 hours) and they cannot impose conditions when forced to release him or her on police bail.

What do the police do after arrest?

After the police have gathered all available evidence and interviewed the abuser the case is then passed to the Crown Prosecution Service (CPS). The CPS decides whether there is enough evidence for a criminal conviction. The CPS applies a number of tests and considers if the matter needs to be resolved in a court of law. If the CPS decides that your case merits action by the courts they will direct the police to charge the person .

What does the term "charging" mean?

Charging in simple language means that a CPS solicitor, after having independently reviewed the evidence before them, believes that the abuser's wrong doing can be realistically proved in a court of law and it is in the public's interest to prosecute the abuser for his or her wrong doing.

What is bail?

Bail is an agreed set of boundaries that the abuser agrees with the police, or court, in order to comply with the criminal justice system. The abuser understands that he or she is free to do whatever they please, however, they must surrender to the court and comply with certain conditions. The conditions that the abuser signs up to are designed to protect both the abuser and the victim.

The police only have the power to impose bail conditions on an arrested person following a charge. The decision to charge someone to court means that the CPS believes that there is enough evidence to prove that the abuser has broken the law.

What type of bail conditions can I ask for?

You will be consulted; however, it is the decision of the police to ensure proportionate conditions are imposed. For example:

- ❏ Not to contact you either directly or indirectly.
- ❏ Not to enter your street or town.
- ❏ Not to drink alcohol.
- ❏ A curfew from 10 pm till 8pm.

You must tell the police how frightened you are.

What is a remand in custody?

Where the crime committed is very serious, and there is evidence that the abuser will not abide by strict bail conditions, the police can apply to hold the abuser in custody. In simple terms the abuser will be held in custody until the court's first hearing. The court will decide whether the abuser is released and given court bail or remanded in custody until the actual court case.

If you haven't been updated you may want to contact the local police station or the nearest magistrates court.

Independent domestic violence advisor

The main purpose of independent domestic violence advisors (IDVAs) is to address your safety. The IDVA will help you implement a plan which addresses immediate safety including practical steps to protect yourself and your children, as well as longer-term solutions. These plans will include actions from the MARAC as well as remedies available through the criminal and civil courts, housing options and services available through other organisations.

What should I do after the abuser has been charged?

After your abuser has been charged it may be a good time to think once again about your safety. Speak to your neighbours and ask them to be vigilant and report matters to the police. Tell the IDVA or police officer that you are concerned about your safety. Ask the police for a copy of the abuser's bail conditions. Revert back to the previous chapter (Safety Plan). If you are still concerned ask the police to apply for a restraining order on conviction. New legislation has just been passed to allow the CPS to apply for a restraining order, even if the court case has been acquitted. This recent piece of legislation may help you get some extra long term protection.

First Hearing

You will be notified of the first court hearing, at this stage you do not need to attend court. This is an opportunity for your abuser to plead guilty at an early stage. If this isn't the case, you will then be notified of a trial date.

Will the abuser or the defence lawyer be given my address?

No, your address is recorded on the front of your statement. Only your statement is given to all persons involved in your case.

Who will read my statement?

Everyone involved with the case will read your statement (eg police, CPS, defence, magistrate or judge).

What if someone tries to intimidate me?

It is a criminal offence to intimidate a witness.

How will I be supported?

You will be appointed a victim care officer. This person will keep you updated about the case and will assess your individual needs. You may receive financial support with regard to childcare arrangements, And travel etc. Victim support can arrange a visit to a court room; this will allow you to get a feel for the entire process. This is a worthwhile experience, as familiarity can allow you to relax and understand the entire process. Your IDVA will also lend a supportive hand prior to attending court and will act as an advocate on your behalf;, any questions, needs or concerns will answered.

What will happen If I don't go to court?

If you have any problems or concerns about going to court, you must inform the witness care officer as soon as possible. The court in certain circumstances issue a summons, that acts as an order to attend.

Going to court

On the actual day get up nice and early and remember to practise a relaxation method before you set of on your journey. This could be as simple as remembering a positive statement or listening to music. Before you leave your home remember to take with you your domestic abuse diary. Arrange to be supported and take a good friend. On arrival make no attempts to look at your abuser or abuser's family. Identify a court room official and ask for the "Prosecution Witness Room". The victim support officer will check you in and you will be asked if you require your written statement. This will serve to refresh your memory. Ask your solicitor or the court usher (the person who tells you to go into the court rooms) what to call the judges. In a Magistrate's Court it is usually Sir or Madam. In other courts it may be Your Honour or Your Lordship/Ladyship. When the judge or magistrate arrives everyone stands up. Watch for what the court people do. Sit down when they do.

Giving Evidence

You will be required to give evidence so that the court can hear what has happened to you. Two solicitors will question you regarding your statement. Firstly the prosecution solicitor will ask you a number of questions. Take your time; you don't have to rush in and answer at once. If you misunderstood the question ask the solicitor to repeat the question. Speak slowly and surely. The defence solicitor will then ask some further questions. Be prepared to be a little unsettled. Again take your time and answer slowly. None of the questioning is aimed at you personally.

Trial events

The court case will be run in chronological order, and after all witnesses have given their evidence it will be the turn of the abuser to answer a number of questions. After all the evidence is heard the magistrate or judge will retire and decide the verdict; either the abuser is guilty or not guilty.

Conviction

Once the court has decided the outcome the abuser will not necessarily be punished on that same day. The court will ask for a number of key agencies to conduct a number of reports. These will form the basis of a pre-sentence report. It may be a number of weeks before the actual punishment or rehabilitation is considered.

7 What the court can do

The courts have a number of powers, they could:

- ❑ Grant a prison sentence.
- ❑ Issue a restraining order.
- ❑ Order the abuser to attend a recognized perpetrator course.
- ❑ Offer the abuser help with alcohol and drug abuse.
- ❑ Order the abuser to pay you a financial sum of money.
- ❑ Order the abuser to do unpaid work in the community.

WHAT IS A PERPETRATOR PROGRAMME?

These are designed to help abusive men stop being violent and abusive and learn how to relate to their partners in a respectful and equal way. Currently there are no perpetrator courses that are aimed at women. Courses run for several weeks and they meet once a week for about two and a half hours in the evening.

There are many different programmes across the UK, and the content will vary, but on the whole they will cover these issues:

- ❑ What is violence and abuse?
- ❑ Understanding why I'm violent.
- ❑ Learning that I am in control of my own behaviour and can choose not to be violent.
- ❑ Taking responsibility for my behaviour, without blaming others or minimising it.
- ❑ Understanding the impact of violence and abuse on my partner and children.
- ❑ Learning how to notice when I am becoming abusive and how to stop.
- ❑ Learning different, non-abusive ways of dealing with difficulties in my relationship.
- ❑ Dealing non-abusively with my partner's anger.
- ❑ Recognising how I get wound up and learning how to wind myself down.
- ❑ Negotiation and listening- how to build a respectful relationship.
- ❑ Some groups are discussion based, but most use a variety of interactive exercises to make the learning realistic, stimulating and relevant to men's own situations.

What is the Criminal Injuries Compensation Authority?

CICA is the government body responsible for administering the Criminal Injuries Compensation Scheme in England, Scotland and Wales.

Victims of violent crime

The CICA provide a free service to victims of violent crime.
Telephone helpline 0800 358 3601

Am I eligible for Criminal Injuries Compensation?

You may be eligible to apply if:

- ❑ You have been injured seriously enough to qualify for at least our minimum award (£1,000).

- ❑ You were injured in an act of violence in England, Scotland or Wales. An offender does not necessarily have to have been convicted of, or even charged with that crime.

- ❑ You have made your application within two years of the incident that caused your injury. (But we might accept applications outside this limit if in your particular case it wasn't reasonable for an application form to have been submitted within two years of the incident and there would still be enough evidence for us to consider.)

But you will not be eligible if:

- ❑ You were injured before 1 August 1964

- ❑ You have already applied for compensation for the same criminal injury, under the 2008 Scheme or under any earlier Scheme operating in England, Scotland and Wales.

- ❑ The injury happened before 1 October 1979 and you and the person who injured you were living together at the time as members of the same family in the same household.

- ❑ The injury and the act of violence took place outside England, Scotland or Wales.

CHAPTER SUMMARY

- ❑ *Tell the police your entire story, don't omit any facts. It's your story.*
- ❑ *Establish the name of the person in charge of your case.*
- ❑ *Tell the police your needs, concerns and expectations.*
- ❑ *Ask the police to apply for a restraining order on conviction.*

8

KEEPING OURSELVES HEALTHY

Domestic Abuse is a stressful, unhealthy experience. Continued abuse impacts not only on your health, but it also affects your children, your relationships with others and the way in which you perceive the world and its daily experiences. This chapter focuses on real achievable holistic health care advice, and places you in the centre. The following sections focus on your physical/emotional and spiritual health. Not all practices may be applicable to you, however feel free to pick and choose a number of practices that you feel comfortable with. Gradually with time, a number of these activities may form the basis of your new life, ensuring that you can cope with minor set backs, daily stresses and bring health and happiness to your self and loved ones. The last section of this chapter is an informative in depth review of Counseling Therapies, Post Traumatic Stress Disorder and Drug and Alcohol Treatments.

If you have been assaulted by your partner, you may need to get treatment straight away, you could call the ambulance service using 999. Be aware that the ambulance service may contact the police as a matter of routine. If you are pregnant or suspect you are pregnant, you must seek urgent medical treatment. You could do this by attending at your local A + E department or ringing your community midwife.

If you have been raped or sexually assaulted, the local authority will usually have a SARC within it's boundaries. For access to this service you could contact the police, women's aid or NHS direct.

SEXUAL ASSAULT REFERRAL CENTRE

A SARC is a one stop location where female and male victims of rape and serious sexual assault can receive medical care and counselling, and have the opportunity to assist the police investigation, including undergoing a forensic examination.

What can a SARC do?

- ❑ Crisis workers to support you after rape and sexual assault.

- ❑ Immediate on-site access to emergency contraception and drugs to prevent sexually transmitted infections including HIV.

- ❑ Integral follow-up services including psycho-social support/counselling, sexual health, and support throughout the criminal justice process.

- ❑ A dedicated, forensically secure facility integrated with hospital services.

- ❑ Availability of forensic examination 24 hours a day, within 4 hours in cases of immediate need.

- ❑ Facilities for self-referrals, including the opportunity to have a forensic examination and for the results to be stored or to be used anonymously. You don't necessarily have to involve the police.

❑ Choice of gender of doctor/forensic medical examiner/appropriately trained Sexual Assault Nurse Examiner. All examiners should be supervised by doctors trained and experienced in sexual assault forensic examination, who can provide interpretation of injuries for criminal justice purposes and ensure the highest standard of forensic examination.

Useful Numbers

NHS Direct **0845 4647** www.nhsdirect.nhs.uk

British Association for Counselling and Psychotherapy **01455 883316** www.bacp.co.uk

Saneline for anyone concerned about their own mental health or that of someone else. Local rate helpline: **08457 678 000** 12 noon to 11pm Monday to Friday and 12 noon to 6pm on Saturday and Sunday. www.sane.org.uk

Samaritans provide a listening service for those in distress or considering suicide. **0845 790 9090** 24 hour helpline.

No Panic: **0808 808 0545** freephone for those suffering from anxiety disorders and panic attacks. Provides advice, counselling, befriending and refers to local services when available.

National self-harm network: www.nshn.co.uk For those who self-harm or for those supporting them. Gives information (and debunks myths) about self harm and lists organisations which provide support.

Rape and Sexual Abuse Support Centre (RASASC) P.O.Box 383, Croydon, CR9 2AW. Helpline: **0845 122 1331**, Open weekdays 12 noon – 2. 30 p.m. and 7.00 p.m. -9.30 p.m.; weekends and bank holidays 2. 30 p.m. – 5 p.m. Minicom: **020 8239 1124** email: info@rasasc.org.uk Website: www.rasasc.org.uk Helpline will take calls from women and men nationwide, and refer to local services if appropriate. Also offers face to face counselling and group counselling for women and men who have been raped or sexually abused, and can travel to Croydon.

Young Minds www.youngminds.org.uk
The Young Minds parents' information service provides support, information and help for parents concerned about a young person's mental health: 0800 018 2138. They also have a variety of leaflets and booklets, including one which explores how divorce and separation affect children and young people.

THE HEALTH NEEDS OF OUR CHILDREN

Younger children may become anxious, complain of tummy-aches or start to wet their bed. They may find it difficult to sleep, have temper tantrums and start to behave as if they are much younger than they are. Older children react differently. Boys seem to express their distress much more outwardly. They may become aggressive and disobedient. Sometimes, they start to use violence to try and solve problems, as if they have learnt to do this from the way that adults behave in their family. Older boys may play truant and may start to use alcohol or drugs.

Girls are more likely to keep their distress inside. They may withdraw from other people and become anxious or depressed. They may think badly of themselves and complain of vague physical symptoms. They are more likely to have an eating disorder, or to harm themselves by taking overdoses or cutting themselves.

Children with these problems often do badly at school. They may also get symptoms of post-traumatic stress disorder, for example have nightmares and flashbacks, and be easily startled.

Are there any long-term effects?

Yes. Children who have witnessed violence are more likely to be either abusers or victims themselves. Children tend to copy the behaviour of their parents. Boys learn from their fathers to be violent to women. Girls learn from their mothers that violence is to be expected, and something you just have to put up with. Children don't always repeat the same pattern when they grow up. Many children don't like what they see, and try very hard not to make the same mistakes as their parents. Even so, children from violent families often grow up feeling anxious and depressed, and find it difficult to get on with other people.

The following section may help you or your family, all the information is researched based and simplified in a short sentence. If you require further information, please seek professional help.

LOOKING AFTER YOUR PHYSICAL BODY

Exercise

Exercise has been proven to lift your mood. You do not have to be super fit as 20 minutes a day is all you need to do. Start slowly and build yourself up.

Seek medical attention

If you have been assaulted, seek medical attention at the earliest opportunity. Take advice from your Doctor/Health Visitor/Midwife.

Try to reduce drinking alcohol

Alcohol is a depressant and will make you feel more depressed the next day. Using alcohol to solve your problems will inevitably lead to further feelings of despair.

Eat regular meals

Eat regular meals that are well balanced and contain the correct nutrients. Breakfast, lunch and tea. Skipping meals adds to fatigue and stress.

Take time off when sick

It's important to rest when we are ill.

Relax

Do not add to your busy life. A good old fashioned day off is just what the doctor ordered. Do the things that comfort you; take a nice hot bath, read a book, eat chocolate, or have a massage.

Take a mini-holiday

Getting away from your troubles will allow you to reflect differently. The solution to life's troubles is sometimes right under our noses and focusing on something else helps us to see things differently.

Get a good night's sleep

After a good night's sleep we begin the day in a better frame of mind. Try and keep to the same routine. Go to bed at 10 pm and rise at about 7 am.

LOOKING AFTER YOUR PSYCHOLOGICAL SELF

Use visualization as a coping tool

When your abuser is particularly nasty visualise them standing as a small clown with a big red nose. Use any type of visualization that helps you make light of a situation.

Make time for self reflection

Write in a journal, draw a picture, consider your inner experiences – listen to your thoughts, judgements, beliefs, attitudes and feelings.

Happiness list

Make a list of all the things that make you feel happy. Carry the list with you and read it once in a while. Focus on the feeling of happiness. Do the things that make you feel happy and treat yourself.

Help others

Helping others helps you. By making someone else's life more pleasurable you gain friendship, support, skills, respect and new opportunities.

LOOKING AFTER YOUR EMOTIONS

Have fun

Be spontaneous and decide to do something new; push your boundaries and enjoy the moment.

Look after your pet

You do not have to own your own pet instead you could walk a neighbour's dog or go and help at the local cattery. Animals offer so much happiness.

Meet new people or start a new hobby

The old saying "A change is as good as a rest" is certainly true. A new direction in life can offer new opportunities. Education is an attitude of mind and helps to broaden your experiences. Look in your local library or town hall. Research groups at your local community centre.

Play music

Classical music works on different levels and has a soothing effect on your mind, body and soul. The power of music is astonishing.

Write poetry

Writing poetry allows us to express our inner feelings and helps us make sense of our world.

Allow yourself to cry

Emotions are best expressed, this can be particularly difficult if you're a man. Crying allows pent up frustrations to be released and can actually improve your inner feelings.

Find things that make you laugh

Humour is an age old anti-dote.

Visit your friends and family

Being around the people who matter to us helps us to reaffirm who we are and what we stand for. Visiting the people who care for us gives us an opportunity to talk and express ourselves.

Re-read favourite books, re-view favourite films

Re-living our inner feelings of happiness allows us to take a break from our current problems.

Give your self praise

Write down the things you do well, in one word describe these qualities.

LOOKING AFTER YOURSELF SPIRITUALLY

Start the day with meditation

Your perception of the world starts with you. Starting the day with a clear mind allows you to concentrate and listen clearer. Qualities such as patience, calmness and tolerance develop. By becoming more centred you co-operate and have the ability to choose your responses to difficult situations.

Walk in the country

The green pastures of the countryside relax and soothe us, and combining the elements with exercise will rejuvenate you. The peace and tranquility of nature has a calming effect.

> **My favorite activities are:**
>
> ....
>
> ....
>
> ....

POST TRAUMATIC STRESS DISORDER

In our everyday lives, any of us can have an experience that is overwhelming, frightening, and beyond our control. Most people, in time, get over experiences like this without needing help. In some people though, traumatic experiences set off a reaction that can last for many months or years. This is called Post- Traumatic Stress Disorder, or PTSD for short.

People who have repeatedly experienced:

- ❏ severe neglect or abuse as an adult or as a child
- ❏ severe repeated violence of abuse as an adult, e.g. torture, abusive imprisonment

can have a similar set of reactions. This is called 'complex PTSD' and is described later in this chapter

How does PTSD start?

PTSD can start after any traumatic event. A traumatic event is one where we can see that we are in danger, our life is threatened, or where we see other people dying or being injured. Some typical traumatic events would be:

❑ violent personal assault (sexual assault, rape, physical attack, abuse, robbery, mugging) Even hearing about an the unexpected injury or violent death of a family member or close friend can start PTSD.

Even hearing about an the unexpected injury or violent death of a family member or close friend can start PTSD.

When does PTSD start?

The symptoms of PTSD can start after a delay of weeks, or even months. They usually appear within 6 months of a traumatic event.

What does PTSD feel like?

Many people feel grief-stricken, depressed, anxious, guilty and angry after a traumatic experience. As well as these understandable emotional reactions, there are three main types of symptoms produced by such an experience:

1. Flashbacks & Nightmares

You find yourself re-living the event, again and again. This can happen both as a "flashback" in the day, and as nightmares when you are asleep. These can be so realistic that it feels as though you are living through the experience all over again. You see it in your mind, but may also feel the emotions and physical sensations of what happened - fear, sweating, smells, sounds, pain.

Ordinary things can trigger off flashbacks. For instance, if you had a car crash in the rain, a rainy day might start a flashback.

It may be so real that you actually believe that your abuser is sitting next to you.

2. Avoidance & Numbing

It can be just too upsetting to re-live your experience over and over again. So you distract yourself. You keep your mind busy by losing yourself in a hobby, working very hard, or spending your time absorbed in crossword or jigsaw puzzles. You avoid places and people that remind you of the trauma, and try not to talk about it.

You may deal with the pain of your feelings by trying to feel nothing at all - by becoming emotionally numb. You communicate less with other people, who then find it hard to live or work with you.

3. Being "On Guard"

You find that you stay alert all the time, as if you are looking out for danger. You can't relax. This is called "hypervigilance". You feel anxious and find it hard to sleep. Other people will notice that you are jumpy and irritable.

Other Symptoms

Emotional reactions to stress are often accompanied by:

- ❑ muscle aches and pains
- ❑ diarrhoea
- ❑ irregular heartbeats
- ❑ headaches
- ❑ feelings of panic and fear
- ❑ depression
- ❑ drinking too much alcohol
- ❑ using drugs (including painkillers).

Why are traumatic events so shocking?

They undermine our sense that life is fair, reasonably safe, and that we are secure. A traumatic experience makes it very clear that we can die at any time. The symptoms of PTSD are part of a normal reaction to narrowly avoided death.

Does everyone get PTSD after a traumatic experience?

No. But nearly everyone will have the symptoms of post traumatic stress for the first month or so. This is because they help to keep you going, and help you to understand the experience you have been through. This is an "acute stress reaction". Over a few weeks, most people slowly come to terms with what has happened, and their stress symptoms start to disappear.

Not everyone is so lucky. About 1 in 3 people will find that their symptoms just carry on and that they can't come to terms with what has happened. It is as though the process has got stuck. The symptoms of post traumatic stress, although normal in themselves, become a problem - or Post Traumatic Stress Disorder - when they go on for too long.

What makes PTSD worse?

The more disturbing the experience, the more likely you are to develop PTSD. The most traumatic events:

- ❑ are sudden and unexpected
- ❑ go on for a long time
- ❑ you are trapped and can't get away
- ❑ involve children.

If you are in a situation where you continue to be exposed to stress and uncertainty, this will make it difficult or impossible for your PTSD symptoms to improve.

What about ordinary "stress"?

Everybody feels stressed from time to time. Unfortunately, the word "stress" is used to mean two rather different things:

❑   our inner sense of worry, feeling tense or feeling burdened. or

❑   the problems in our life that are giving us these feelings. This could be

work, relationships, maybe just trying to get by without much money. Unlike PTSD, these things are with us, day in and day out. They are part of normal, everyday life, but can produce anxiety, depression, tiredness, and headaches. They can also make some physical problems worse, such as stomach ulcers and skin problems. These are certainly troublesome, but they are not the same as PTSD.

Why does PTSD happen?

We don't know for certain. There are a several possible explanations for why PTSD occurs.

Psychological

When we are frightened, we remember things very clearly. Although it can be distressing to remember these things, it can help us to understand what happened and, in the long run, help us to survive.

❑   The flashbacks, or replays, force us to think about what has happened. We can decide what to do if it happens again. After a while, we learn to think about it without becoming upset.

❑   It is tiring and distressing to remember a trauma. Avoidance and numbing keep the number of replays down to a manageable level.

❑   Being "on guard" means that we can react quickly if another crisis happens.

But we don't want to spend the rest of our life going over it. We only want to think about it when we have to - if we find ourselves in a similar situation.

How do I know when I've got over a traumatic experience?

When you can:

❑   think about it without becoming distressed

❑   not feel constantly under threat

❑   not think about it at inappropriate times.

Why is PTSD often not recognised?

❑   None of us like to talk about upsetting events and feelings.

❑	We may not want to admit to having symptoms, because we don't wantto be thought of as weak or mentally unstable.

❑	Doctors and other professionals are human. They may feel uncomfortable if we try to talk about gruesome or horrifying events.

❑	People with PTSD often find it easier to talk about the other problems that go along with it - headache, sleep problems, irritability, depression, tension, substance abuse, family or work-related problems.

How can I tell if I have PTSD?

Have you have experienced a traumatic event of the sort described at the start of this leaflet?

If you have, do you:

❑	have vivid memories, flashbacks or nightmares?

❑	avoid things that remind you of the event?

❑	feel emotionally numb at times?

❑	feel irritable and constantly on edge but can't see why?

❑	eat more than usual, or use more drink or drugs than usual?

❑	feel out of control of your mood?

❑	find it more difficult to get on with other people?

❑	have to keep very busy to cope?

❑	feel depressed or exhausted?

If it is less that 6 weeks since the traumatic event, and these experiences are slowly improving, they may be part of the normal process of adjustment.

If it is more than 6 weeks since the event, and these experiences don't seem to be getting better, it is worth talking it over with your doctor.

Children and PTSD

PTSD can develop at any age.

Younger children may have upsetting dreams of the actual trauma, which then change into nightmares of monsters. They often re-live the trauma in their play. For example, a child involved in a serious road traffic accident might re- enact the crash with toy cars, over and over again.

They may lose interest in things they used to enjoy. They may find it hard to believe that they will live long enough to grow up.

They often complain of stomach aches and headaches.

8 How can PTSD be helped?

Helping yourself

Do ....

- ❑ keep life as normal as possible
- ❑ get back to your usual routine
- ❑ talk about what happened to someone you trust
- ❑ try relaxation exercises
- ❑ go back to work
- ❑ eat and exercise regularly
- ❑ go back to where the traumatic event happened
- ❑ take time to be with family and friends
- ❑ drive with care - your concentration may be poor
- ❑ be more careful generally - accidents are more likely at this time
- ❑ speak to a doctor
- ❑ expect to get better.

Don't ....

- ❑ beat yourself up about it - PTSD symptoms are not a sign of weakness. They are a normal reaction, of normal people, to terrifying experiences
- ❑ bottle up your feelings. If you have developed PTSD symptoms, don't keep it to yourself because treatment is usually very successful.
- ❑ avoid talking about it.
- ❑ expect the memories to go away immediately, they may be with you for quite some time.
- ❑ expect too much of yourself. Cut yourself a bit of slack while you adjust to what has happened.
- ❑ stay away from other people.
- ❑ drink lots of alcohol or coffee or smoke more.
- ❑ get overtired.
- ❑ miss meals.
- ❑ take holidays on your own.

What can interfere with getting better?

You may find that other people will:

- ❑ not let you talk about it
- ❑ avoid you

- ❑ be angry with you
- ❑ think of you as weak
- ❑ blame you

These are all ways in which other people protect themselves from thinking about gruesome or horrifying events. It won't help you because it doesn't give you the chance to talk over what has happened to you.

You may not be able to talk easily about it. A traumatic event can put you into a trance-like state which makes the situation seem unreal or bewildering. It is harder to deal with if you can't remember what happened, can't put it into words, or can't make sense of it.

Treatment

Just as there are both physical and psychological aspects to PTSD, so there are both physical and psychological treatments for it.

Psychotherapy

All the effective psychotherapies for PTSD focus on the traumatic experiences that have produced your symptoms rather than your past life. You cannot change or forget what has happened. You can learn to think differently about it, about the world, and about your life.

You need to be able to remember what happened, as fully as possible, without being overwhelmed by fear and distress. These therapies help you to put words to the traumatic experiences that you have had. By remembering the event, going over it and making sense of it, your mind can do its normal job, of storing the memories away and moving on to other things.

If you can start to feel safe again and in control of your feelings, you won't need to avoid the memories as much. Indeed, you can gain more control over your memories so that you only think about them when you want to, rather than having them erupt into your mind spontaneously.

All these treatments should all be given by specialists in the treatment of PTSD. The sessions should be at least weekly, every week, with the same therapist, and should usually continue for 8-12 weeks. Although sessions will usually last around an hour, they may sometimes last up to 90 minutes.

Cognitive Behavioural Therapy (CBT) is a way of helping you to think differently about your memories, so that they become less distressing and more manageable. It will usually also involve some relaxation work to help you tolerate the discomfort of thinking about the traumatic events.

EMDR (Eye Movement Desensitisation & Reprocessing) is a technique which uses eye movements to help the brain to process flashbacks and to make sense of the traumatic experience. It may sound odd, but it has been shown to work. Within the sphere of treating trauma, this technique is regarded as the most effective.

Group therapy involves meeting with a group of other people who have been through the same, or a similar traumatic event. The fact that other people in the group do have some idea of what you have been through can make it much easier to talk about what has happened.

Medication

SSRI antidepressant tablets will both reduce the strength of PTSD symptoms and relieve any depression that is also present. They will need to be prescribed by a doctor.

This type of medication should not make you sleepy, although they all have some side-effects in some people. They may also produce unpleasant symptoms if stopped quickly, so the dose should usually be reduced gradually. If they are helpful, you should carry on taking them for around 12 months. Soon after starting an antidepressany, some people may find that they feel more:

❑ anxious
❑ restless
❑ suicidal

Occasionally, if someone is so distressed that they cannot sleep or think clearly, anxiety-reducing medication may be necessary. These tablets should usually not be prescribed for more than 10 days or so.

Body-focussed Therapies

These can help to control the distress of PTSD. They can also reduce hyperarousal, or the feeling of being "on guard" all the time. These therapies include physiotherapy and osteopathy, but also complementary therapies such as massage, acupuncture, reflexology, yoga, meditation and tai chi. They all help you to develop ways of relaxing and managing stress.

Effectiveness of Treatments

At present, there is evidence that EMDR, cognitive behavioural therapy and antidepressants are all effective. There is not enough information for us to say that one of these treatments is better than another. There is no evidence that other forms of psychotherapy or counselling are helpful to PTSD.

Complex PTSD

This can start weeks or months after the traumatic event, but may take years to be recognised for what they are. As well as the symptoms of PTSD described above, you may:

- ❏ feel shame and guilt
- ❏ have a sense of numbness, a lack of feelings in your body
- ❏ be unable to enjoy anything
- ❏ control your emotions by using street drugs, alcohol, or by harmingyourself
- ❏ cut yourself off from what is going on around you (dissociation)
- ❏ have physical symptoms caused by your distress
- ❏ find that you can't put your emotions into words
- ❏ want to kill yourself
- ❏ take risks and do things on the 'spur of the moment'.

What makes PTSD worse?

If:

- ❏ it happens at an early stage - the earlier the age, the worse the trauma
- ❏ it is caused by a parent or other care giver
- ❏ the trauma is severe
- ❏ the trauma goes on for a long time
- ❏ you are isolated
- ❏ you are still in touch with the abuser and/or threats to your safety.

How does it come about?

The earlier the trauma happens, the more it affects psychological development. Some children cope by being defensive or aggressive, while others cut themselves off from what is going on around them. They tend to grow up with a sense of shame and guilt rather than feeling confident and good about themselves.

Getting better

Try to start doing the normal things of life that have nothing to do with your past experiences of trauma. This could include finding friends, getting a job, doing regular exercise, learning relaxation techniques, developing a hobby or having pets. This helps you slowly to trust the world around you.

Lack of trust in other people - and the world in general - is central to complex PTSD. Treatment often needs to be longer to allow you to develop a secure relationship with a therapist - if you like, to experience that it is possible to trust someone in this world without being abused. The work will often happen in 3 stages:

Stabilisation

You learn how to understand and control your distress and emotional cutting off, or 'dissociation'. This can involve 'grounding' techniques to help you stay in the present

- concentrating on ordinary physical feelings that remind you that you are not still living in the traumatic past.

You may also be able to 'disconnect' your physical symptoms of fear and anxiety from the memories and emotions that produce them, making them less frightening.

You start to be able to tolerate day to day life without experiencing anxiety and flashbacks. This may sometimes be the only help that is needed.

Trauma-focused Therapy

EMDR or CBT (see above) can help you remember your traumatic experiences with less distress and more control. Other psychotherapies, including psychodynamic psychotherapy, can also be helpful. Care needs to be taken in complex PTSD because these treatments can make the situation worse if not used properly.

Reintegration

You begin to develop a new life for yourself. You become able to use your skills or learn new ones and to make satisfying relationships in the real world.

Medication can be used if you feel too distressed or unsafe, or if psychotherapy is not possible. It can include both antidepressants and antipsychotioc medication - but not usually tranquillisers or sleeping tablets.

WHAT IS CBT?

It is a way of talking about:

- ❑ How you think about yourself, the world and other people
- ❑ How what you do affects your thoughts and feelings.

CBT can help you to change how you think ("Cognitive") and what you do ("Behaviour"). These changes can help you to feel better. Unlike some of the other talking treatments, it focuses on the "here and now" problems and difficulties. Instead of focussing on the causes of your distress or symptoms in the past, it looks for ways to improve your state of mind now.

It has been found to be helpful in Anxiety, Depression, Panic, Agoraphobia and other phobias, Social phobia, Bulimia, Obsessive compulsive disorder, Post traumatic stress disorder and Schizophrenia

How does it work?

CBT can help you to make sense of overwhelming problems by breaking them down into smaller parts. This makes it easier to see how they are connected and how they affect you. These parts are:

- ❑ A Situation - a problem, event or difficult situation

From this can follow:

❏ Thoughts
❏ Emotions
❏ Physical feelings
❏ Actions

Each of these areas can affect the others. How you think about a problem can affect

Example:

	Unhelpful	Helpful
Situation:	You've had a bad day, feel fed up, so go out shopping. As you walk down the road, someone you know walks by and, apparently, ignores you.	
Thoughts:	He/she ignored me - they don't like me	He/she looks a bit wrapped up in themselves - I wonder if there's something wrong?
Emotional: **Feelings**	Low, sad and rejected	Concerned for the other person
Physical:	Stomach cramps, low energy, feel sick	None - feel comfortable
Action:	Go home and avoid them	Get in touch to make sure they're OK

how you feel physically and emotionally. It can also alter what you do about it. There are helpful and unhelpful ways of reacting to most situations, depending on how you think about them.

The same situation has led to two very different results, depending on how you thought about the situation. How you **think** has affected how you **felt** and what you **did**. In the example in the left hand column, you've jumped to a conclusion without very much evidence for it - and this matters, because it's led to:

❏ a number of uncomfortable feelings
❏ an unhelpful behaviour.

If you go home feeling depressed, you'll probably brood on what has happened and

103

feel worse. If you get in touch with the other person, there's a good chance you'll

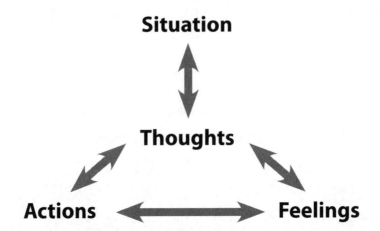

feel better about yourself. If you don't, you won't have the chance to correct any misunderstandings about what they think of you - and you will probably feel worse. This is a simplified way of looking at what happens. The whole sequence, and parts of it, can also feedback like this:

This "vicious circle" can make you feel worse. It can even create new situations that make you feel worse. You can start to believe quite unrealistic (and unpleasant) things about yourself. This happens because, when we are distressed, we are more likely to jump to conclusions and to interpret things in extreme and unhelpful ways.

CBT can help you to break this vicious circle of altered thinking, feelings and behaviour. When you see the parts of the sequence clearly, you can change them - and so change the way you feel. CBT aims to get you to a point where you can "do it yourself", and work out your own ways of tackling these problems.

"Five areas" assessment

This is another way of connecting all the 5 areas mentioned above. It builds in our relationships with other people and helps us to see how these can make us feel better or worse. Other issues such as debt, job and housing difficulties are also important. If you improve one area, you are likely to improve other parts of your life as well.

What does CBT involve?

The sessions

CBT can be done individually or with a group of people. It can also be done from a self-help book or computer programme. In England and Wales two computer-based programmes have been approved for use by the NHS. Fear Fighter is for people with phobias or panic attacks, Beating the Blues is for people with mild to moderate depression.

If you have individual therapy:

- ❑ You will usually meet with a therapist for between 5 and 20, weekly, or fortnightly, sessions. Each session will last between 30 and 60 minutes.
- ❑ In the first 2-4 sessions, the therapist will check that you can use this sort of treatment and you will check that you feel comfortable with it.
- ❑ The therapist will also ask you questions about your past life and background. Although CBT concentrates on the here and now, at times you may need to talk about the past to understand how it is affecting you now.
- ❑ You decide what you want to deal with in the short, medium and long term.
- ❑ You and the therapist will usually start by agreeing on what to discuss that day.

The work

- ❑ With the therapist, you break each problem down into its separate parts, as in the example above. To help this process, your therapist may ask you to keep a diary. This will help you to identify your individual patterns of thoughts, emotions, bodily feelings and actions.
- ❑ Together you will look at your thoughts, feelings and behaviours to work out:
  - if they are unrealistic or unhelpful
  - how they affect each other, and you.
- ❑ The therapist will then help you to work out how to change unhelpful thoughts and behaviours
- ❑ It's easy to talk about doing something, much harder to actually do it. So, after you have identified what you can change, your therapist will recommend "homework" - you practise these changes in your everyday life. Depending on the situation, you might start to:
- ❑ Question a self-critical or upsetting thought and replace it with a positive (and more realistic) one that you have developed in CBT
- ❑ recognise that you are about to do something that will make you feel worse and, instead, do something more helpful.
- ❑ At each meeting you discuss how you've got on since the last session. Your therapist can help with suggestions if any of the tasks seem too hard or don't seem to be helping.
- ❑ They will not ask you to do things you don't want to do - you decide the pace of the treatment and what you will and won't try. The strength of CBT is that you can continue to practise and develop your skills even after the sessions have finished. This makes it less likely that your symptoms or problems will return.

How effective is CBT?

- ❑ It is one of the most effective treatments for conditions where anxiety or depression is the main problem

❑ It is the most effective psychological treatment for moderate and severe depression

❑ It is as effective as antidepressants for many types of depression

What other treatments are there and how do they compare?

CBT is used in many conditions, so it isn't possible to list them all in this leaflet. We will look at alternatives to the most common problems - anxiety and depression.

❑ CBT isn't for everyone and another type of talking treatment may work better for you.

❑ CBT is as effective as antidepressants for many forms of depression. It may be slightly more effective than antidepressants in treating anxiety.

❑ For severe depression, CBT should be used with antidepressant medication. When you are very low you may find it hard to change the way you think until antidepressants have started to make you feel better.

❑ Tranquillisers should not be used as a long term treatment for anxiety. CBT is a better option.

Problems with CBT

❑ If you are feeling low and are having difficulty concentrating, it can be hard, at first, to get the hang of CBT - or, indeed, any psychotherapy

❑ This may make you feel disappointed or overwhelmed. A good therapist will pace your sessions so you can cope with the work you are trying to do

❑ It can sometimes be difficult to talk about feelings of depression, anxiety, shame or anger

How long will the treatment last?

A course may be from 6 weeks to 6 months. It will depend on the type of problem and how it is working for you. The availability of CBT varies between different areas and there may be a waiting list for treatment.

What if the symptoms come back?

There is always a risk that the anxiety or depression will return. If they do, your CBT skills should make it easier for you to control them. So, it is important to keep practising your CBT skills, even after you are feeling better.

There is some research that suggests CBT may be better than antidepressants at preventing depression coming back. If necessary, you can have a "refresher" course.

So what impact would CBT have on my life?

Depression and anxiety are unpleasant. They can seriously affect your ability to work and enjoy life. CBT can help you to control the symptoms. It is unlikely to have a negative effect on your life, apart from the time you need to give up to do it.

PSYCHOTHERAPY

There are many different types of psychotherapy. They are all ways of helping people to overcome stress, emotional problems, relationship problems or troublesome habits. What they have in common is that they are all treatments based on talking to another person and sometimes doing things together. They are the "talking treatments". The person carrying out the treatment is usually called a therapist, the person being seen is usually referred to as the client.

Psychodynamic psychotherapy

This focuses on the feelings we have about other people, especially our family and those we are close to. Treatment involves discussing past experiences and how these may have led to our present situation and also how these past experiences may be affecting our life now. The understanding gained frees the person to make choices about what happens in the future.

Psychodynamic psychotherapy may involve quite brief therapy for specific difficulties. If your problems are long-standing, treatment may mean attending regular sessions over many months.

Behavioural psychotherapy

This tries to change patterns of behaviour more directly. Patients can be helped to overcome fears by spending more and more time in the situation they fear, or by learning ways of reducing their anxiety. They may be given 'homework' exercises, and asked to keep diaries or to practice new skills between sessions.

Behavioural psychotherapy is particularly effective for anxiety, panic, phobias, obsessive-compulsive problems and various kinds of social or sexual difficulty. Relief from symptoms often occurs quite quickly.

Can these different approaches work together?

These are all very different sorts of treatment, but they all help us to understand better how we work, which can help us to make changes in our lives.

Psychotherapists may use a combination of techniques to suit the individual, and people may progress from say individual to group therapy, or marital work to individual treatment.

What actually happens?

Psychotherapy usually involves regular meetings at the same time, same place every week or two weeks. In most cases the length of the treatment will be agreed between the client(s) and the therapist(s) within a month or so of starting. What happens during a session is usually considered confidential to the people in that session.

In individual psychotherapy, one patient and one therapist talk together in a quiet room, usually for 50 minutes or so.

In group therapy, several people with similar sorts of problems meet regularly with a therapist or therapists. These sessions may be longer than in individual psychotherapy. Group therapy may appear less intimate, but it is not a cheap or second-rate treatment - in fact it is the best treatment for some problems. The experience of discovering one is not alone, and of being able to help other people, is powerfully encouraging and is often the first step towards getting better.

COUNSELLING

Counselling takes place when a counsellor sees a client in a private and confidential setting to explore a difficulty the client is having, distress they may be experiencing or perhaps their dissatisfaction with life, or loss of a sense of direction and purpose. It is always at the request of the client as no one can properly be 'sent' for counselling.

Confidentiality may be examined if there is a serious danger of harm to someone - either the person or someone else, counsellors may consider whether it is necessary to discuss this with someone else (e.g. a G.P). Normal practice is for the counsellor to share their concern with the client concerned and for the client and counsellor together to consider what, if anything, it might be helpful to share, and with whom.

By listening attentively and patiently the counsellor can begin to perceive the difficulties from the client's point of view and can help them to see things more clearly, possibly from a different perspective.

Counselling is a way of enabling choice or change or of reducing confusion. It does not involve giving advice or directing a client to take a particular course of action. Counsellors do not judge or exploit their clients in any way.

In the counselling sessions the client can explore various aspects of their life and feelings, talking about them freely and openly in a way that is rarely possible with friends or family. Bottled up feelings such as anger, anxiety, grief and embarrassment can become very intense and counselling offers an opportunity to explore them, with the possibility of making them easier to understand. The counsellor will encourage the expression of feelings and as a result of their training will be able to accept and reflect the client's problems without becoming burdened by them.

Acceptance and respect for the client are essentials for a counsellor and, as the relationship develops, so too does trust between the counsellor and client, enabling the client to look at many aspects of their life, their relationships and themselves which they may not have considered or been able to face before.

The counsellor may help the client to examine in detail the behaviour or situations which are proving troublesome and to find an area where it would be possible to initiate some change as a start. The counsellor may help the client to look at the options open to them and help them to decide the best for them.

Counselling or psychotherapy training?

It is not possible to make a generally accepted distinction between counselling and psychotherapy. There are well founded traditions which use the terms interchangeably and others which distinguish between them. If there are differences, then they relate more to the individual psychotherapist's or counsellor's training and interests and to the setting in which they work, rather than to any intrinsic difference in the two activities. to offer therapeutic work which in any other context would be called psychotherapy.

WHAT IS MEDITATION?

Meditation is the practice of focussing your mind on a positive, virtuous feeling. For example if you are feeling bitter and resentful and you focus your meditation on the feeling of love. After spending time concentrating on the feeling of love, your mind will feel more peaceful. Meditation has its origins in many of the world's religions. It is a technique and there is not a right way or wrong way to meditate. The goal of meditation is to train the mind to think more positively.

What are the benefits of meditation?

Meditation has been scrutinized by many scientific studies. It has been proven that the technique of meditation can reduce stress and improve relaxation.

How do I meditate?

Meditate in a clear and quiet place. Do not rush straight into the meditation but spend a few moments to relax into a comfortable posture with your back straight but not tense. Always begin by developing a positive wish to benefit yourself and others through your meditation. Try not to forget the objective meditation. The objective is the type of feeling you are trying to focus on. Before you rise from meditation, mentally dedicate the positive energy that you have created to yourself and others. Throughout the day try and recall the feeling of meditation as often as you can. Use it to guide everything you think, say and do. Spend twenty minutes each day meditating.

What can I expect?

The practice of meditation will take some time to master, and take each session slowly. Meditation is a skill that can be learnt. Like all skills you have to practice them daily. Do not be hard on yourself in the early days. You will get glimpses of a peaceful mind, however, with time and effort the experience of peace will lengthen.

An actual meditation – "Breathing Meditation"

Sit on a chair in quiet a room by yourself. Unplug the phone and give yourself twenty minutes of uninterrupted time. Keep your feet firmly on the floor. Place your hands in a cupped position and find a relaxed position with your back straight. Close your eyes. Take a deep breath and count in your head to the number four. Exhale with a long relaxed breath and count to the number six. Continue with this until you are feeling a little more relaxed. Spend five minutes breathing deeply. Thoughts will keep whizzing into your head. Don't try and stop them but let them come and go. Thoughts are like the tide; they come in and go out. Try not to let the tide sweep you out to sea. Continue to focus on your breath. As you inhale feel the cool air pass your nostrils, and as you exhale feel the warm air pass through your nostrils. Focus on the feelings of cold air and warm air. Continue breathing deeply for six counts and exhaling for six counts. Try and hold your concentration for five minutes. Within this breathing meditation we are aiming to focus on the feeling air. Relax and breathe. As you relax maintain your concentration.

As you inhale imagine the breath as white smoke entering your body, helping you and nourishing every cell in your body. As you exhale imagine thick black smoke leaving your body, making you more rejuvenated and stronger. Imagine that you are slowly cleansing your mind. Visualise your pure heart and feel at peace with yourself. Slowly resume by concentrating on your breath, enjoying that space of calm and happiness. Open your eyes."

A meditation to oppose anger - focussing and harvesting a loving mind meditation

Sit on a chair in a quiet room by yourself. Unplug the phone and give yourself twenty minutes of uninterrupted time. Keep your feet firmly on the floor. Place your hands in a cupped position and find a relaxed position with your back straight. Close your eyes. Take a deep breath and count in your head to the number four. Exhale with a long relaxed breath and count to the number six. Continue with this until you are feeling a little more relaxed. Spend five minutes breathing deeply. Today there are many people who exist to benefit you and do so to ensure all your happiness. Believe it or not, but kindness is all around us. Every act that a person does has at the heart of it an act of kindness or goodness. Starting with you, I want you to consider the kindness that you have received. As you read through the following descriptions I want you to think about your own life and feel each person's happiness. The clothes you are wearing were the result of someone else's happiness. Many people were involved in making the clothes in harsher conditions than you are living in. Roads were built to help transport the clothes. The roads were built by hard physical work in very demanding circumstances. The labourers were working for their happiness and yours. Eventually the clothes were displayed in a shop. You were given money so that you could purchase them. The room you are sitting in was constructed to provide your family with shelter and security. The architect, the builder, the carpenter, the plasterer all co- operated to provide you with this basic need. The meal you ate last passed through many hands before you ate it. The farmer, the packager, the cook all worked together to feed you. They did this to provide happiness to themselves and others. Happiness is born out of love. The book you are reading was given to you as others want you to be happy. Your family spent hours teaching you to read and sent you to school. The teacher taught you many skills so that you can co-operate in this world. All your daily needs have been taken care off. Somebody somewhere has considered your problems and has provided a solution to your suffering. We have central heating, clean sanitation, medicines, charities, transportation, education, music, etc. All that is around us has been provided by many people. Indeed I have written this book as I genuinely want you to be happy. Focus on feeling and understanding that others have acted as a result of love. As you visualise all this kindness focus on the feeling of love that is developing in your heart. Now keep and hold the feeling of love within your heart until it begins to fade away. As it fades away remind yourself about how many people have benefited you and acted out of love, once again focus and concentrate on the feeling of love. As you rise out of the meditation return to focussing on your breath, imagine all your anger slowly rising in the air as thick black smoke. As you take a breath imagine pure light entering every part of your body.

A Meditation To Heal Life's Problems

This powerful meditation is also know as "taking and giving". It is a meditation that heals and restores. "I want you to imagine in your mind all the problems, anxieties and fears that you have about the bullying that you are experiencing. Picture the people, circumstances and situations clearly. Remind yourself about the hurt that you have been feeling and the emotions that have accumulated in your heavy heart. Now imagine rising above all this hurt and clearly seeing all that has happened to you. Slowly imagine turning these visions into thick black smoke. As you take a deep breath in, imagine all the black smoke entering your body. The smoke clears as it enters your heart and dissolves. Now as you exhale imagine sending rays of warm, pure light from your heart breaking all the unhappiness in the world. Send as much light to as many people as you can. Continue to use this visualisation as you breathe in and out. Focus your concentration on this meditation for as long as you can" There are many forms of meditation. Meditation can be used to improve your mental happiness. Try different styles of meditation and experiment with the one that suits your particular needs. Some styles focus on a particular religious aspect and others do not. It is entirely up to you.

DRUG AND ALCOHOL HEALTHCARE

Many people who have experienced Domestic Abuse have also developed a need to use Drugs and Alcohol. Research confirms these fact's. You may have noticed a need to have a stiff drink after an unpleasant experience. After time the need to drink or use drugs has become a daily habit. There are many statutory and voluntary agencies that understand your experience and can help using various approaches. There are many reasons why some one uses substances: escapism, pain removal, coping ability and doing what others tell them.

Where can I get help?

A good website that lists all agencies in the UK is the Alcohol Concern Website: servicesdirectory.alcoholconcern.org.uk/

Talk to frank 0800 77 66 00 www.talktofrank.com

Drink line is also useful **0800 917 8282**

You may also find information from **NHS Direct, Citizen's Advice Bureau** or your local **Women's Aid** Outreach Worker.

Approaching a Local Agency

When you walk through the door of a local agency, you will first be given an explanation of what the agency can offer you depending on your personal circumstances. The counsellor or therapist will sit down with you in a closed room, whereby you will be asked a number of questions. Confidentiality may be examined if there is a serious danger of harm to someone - either the person or someone else, counsellors may consider whether it is necessary to discuss this with someone else (e.g. a G.P). Normal practice is for the counsellor to share their concern with the client concerned and for the client and counsellor together to consider what, if anything, it might be helpful to share, and with whom. The questions will ask you about your personal life, your drinking / drugs habits and your willingness to participate in a programme of change. The counsellor will not expect you to have the answers and will listen and not judge your answers. Many counsellor's have had domestic violence training and are aware of your complex situation.

Once the counsellor has built a detailed picture of your current lifestyle and habits, the counsellor will design a care plan that suits your needs. You may be asked to sign a contract that summarises your individual care plan. If you are drinking or using heavily it is advisable not to stop drinking / using straight away. A slow reduction plan is generally followed.

What can I expect?

The methods used vary from agency to agency, however you may be offered a detailed 12 steps programme incorporating the following:

- ❏ One to One Counselling (Choice of male or female counsellor)
- ❏ Group Sessions (may not be appropriate for Domestic Violence)
- ❏ Medication (this may put you more danger, depending on the type of medication, if in doubt ask.)
- ❏ An education programme (understanding alcohol and drugs)
- ❏ Herbal Medication (helping you sleep, detoxification)
- ❏ Ear Acupunture (helps to reduce stress and cravings)
- ❏ Out Reach Work (a worker will help you with needle exchange etc)
- ❏ Post Counselling Groups (A chance to support others)
- ❏ Other processes such as Cognitive Behavioral Therapy.

Please note not all agencies follow a 12 step method of treatment and may mix and match various treatments.

9

THE SCOPE OF DOMESTIC ABUSE

9 The scope of domestic abuse

Domestic abuse affects different people from all walks of life and it is not confined to one group of people. The complexity of the far reaching effects of domestic abuse cannot be fully explained within the context of this book. The society in which we live is diverse and rich with culture and past times that span the whole world. The needs of different communities are best answered by people who understand the communities in which they have grown up in and understand. The following organisations can help you with regard to your personal circumstances.

Forced Marriage

If you fear you may be forced into marriage overseas, or know someone else who may be, the Forced Marriage Unit may be able to help. You could call one of the following numbers: **020 7008 0230**, **020 7008 0135** or **020 7008 8706**. You can also contact them at **fmu@fco.gov.uk**. All calls and emails are dealt with on a totally confidential basis by skilled caseworkers who are fully aware of the cultural, social and emotional issues surrounding this abuse.

Minority Communities

Black Association of Women Step Out

Cardiff Address:
9 Cathedral Road
Cardiff
CF11 9HA
Tel: **02920 644633**
Fax: 02920 644588
www.bawso.org.uk

Southall Black Sisters

Resource centre mainly for Asian, African, and Afro-Caribbean women. They provide advice and information on domestic violence, racial harassment, welfare, immigration rights, and matrimonial rights. They provide face to face support and case work for women in the London Borough of Ealing but also deal with enquiries on a national basis. Telephone: **0208 571 9595**; email: **sbs@leonet.co.uk** Website: **www.southallblacksisters.org.uk**

Apna Ghar 0207 474 1547 - 24 hours, every day. A helpline for Asian women experiencing domestic violence. Languages spoken include: Bengali, Hindi, Punjabi, Gujarati, Tamil and Urdu.

Asian Women's Helpline 0800 052 6077* Monday – Thursday 9 a.m. – 5. 30 p.m; Fridays 9 a.m. – 5 p.m. For Asian women experiencing domestic violence, as well as other issues. Languages spoken: Bengali, Hindi, Punjabi and Urdu.

Chinese Information and Advice Centre

For Chinese people on a low income, or who have difficulty communicating in English to access mainstream support services. Domestic Violence Line: **0207 462 1281**; Legal Advice Line: **0207 462 1285**.

Turkish Cypriot Women's Project

Telephone: **0208 340 3300**

Offers help with emergency housing, children, injunctions against violent partners, welfare benefits, healthcare matters and other issues related to domestic violence. They provide a free service for any Turkish-speaking woman living in London.

Jewish Women's Aid

Provides a number of different services including a helpline, floating support and outreach for Jewish women and their children. London based. Telephone: **0208 445 8060** Monday – Friday, 9 a.m. – 5 p.m.

Latin American Women's Aid

Provides refuge accommodation, a helpline and outreach for Latin American women and children experiencing domestic violence. Staff speak Spanish, Portuguese and Russian. London based. Telephone: **0207 275 0321** Monday to Friday 9.30 a.m. – 6 p.m.

LGBT

Broken Rainbow is a charity dedicated to supporting lesbian, gay, bisexual and transgender people who are experiencing domestic violence. The service manages a helpline, and also advises mainstream organisations, and offers training on LGBT issues. The Broken Rainbow National Helpline offers a UK wide confidential service giving information, support and advice on legal and housing options, safety and home security, and will make referrals to other services as appropriate. Ring the Helpline on **08452 604460**, minicom **0207 231 3884**; **http://www.broken-rainbow.org.uk/**

Galop works to prevent and challenge homophobic and transphobic hate crime in Greater London. They reduce crimes against lesbian, gay, bisexual and transgender people, and campaign for an improved criminal justice system. Helpline: **020 7704 2040** email: **info@galop.org.uk** **www.galop.org.uk**

10

MOVING
ON

10 Moving on

It may be that your life is slowly improving and that you are starting to feel adjusted to a new life, free from violence and abuse. You have every right to feel proud of your achievements. The decision to confront domestic abuse is one that indicates bravery, courage and determination. The decision to improve your circumstances has great benefits for future generations of your family. The future begins with a slow, methodical step in the next direction. Your experience of domestic abuse will have tired your body and mind to near exhaustion. Take your time each day. The healing process will take a number of months. Now is the time again to refocus on your health.

SUPPORT

Make a **S**afety Plan.

Understand that it is not your fault.

Preserve evidence, write about your experiences.

Protect yourself legally; take advice from civil and criminal solicitors. Apply for a non-molestation order or a restraining order.

Organise support from many agencies; many people can help you.

Respect your health; it will help you keep strong.

Talk to someone; express your feelings.

All personal safety products listed within this book can be purchased from www.the-bully.com. Consider you online safety when ordering from this website.

Bullied Publications also produce an excellent book for teenagers who are experiencing bullying at home, work or school.

Bullied

A survivor's handbook for people affected by domestic violence, school bullying and workplace bullying.

Neville Evans

Notes